EUROPEAN JOURNAL OF WORK AND ORGANIZATIONAL PSYCHOLOGY, 1998, 7 (4), 449–454

Expertise at Work: Research Perspectives and Practical Interventions for Ensuring Excellent Performance at the Workplace

Sabine Sonnentag

University of Amsterdam, The Netherlands

Ute Schmidt-Braße

PSYCON, Wildeshausen, Germany

At this moment, work and its organization are undergoing dramatic changes. Globalization, increased use of information and communication technologies, organizational development and restructuring are some keywords in this ongoing change process. It is assumed that knowledge and employees' competencies will belong to the core resources in these future work organizations (cf. Lawler & Ledford, 1997). This implies that excellent individual and organizational level performance will highly depend on knowledge, other competencies, and their efficient application in the work process. In this context, work and organizational psychologists face a number of challenging research and implementation questions:

- How do excellent performers proceed when accomplishing tasks, and which strategies do they use?
- Which aspects of knowledge and behaviour are crucial for excellent job performance?
- How can excellent performers be identified, selected, and trained?

This Special Issue addresses these questions and presents empirical studies and practitioners' approaches to these challenging issues. We discuss the topic under the heading "Expertise"—a concept that points to high and excellent performance and focuses on knowledge and process aspects underlying high performance.

Requests for reprints should be addressed to S. Sonnentag, Dept. of Psychology, University of Amsterdam, Roetersstraat 15, NL-1018 WB Amsterdam, The Netherlands; Email: ao_sonnentag@macmail.psy.uva.nl

T0347246

THE EXPERTISE CONCEPT

The terms *expert* and *expertise* have a variety of meanings both in everyday language and in scientific research. The expertise concept we adopt for this Special Issue is based on the work of Ericsson and Smith (1991) who characterized the goal of expertise research to "understand and account for what distinguishes outstanding individuals in a domain from less outstanding individuals in that domain, as well as from people in general" (p. 2). Thus, we conceptualize expertise as high and excellent performance in a specific domain. High performance should show a certain degree of stability across time and should be clearly attributable to characteristics of the person—as opposed to just chance or good luck.

This conceptualization differs from that used in many existing studies mainly conducted in the field of cognitive psychology. In these studies, expertise has been equated with years of experience: Persons with a long experience were "automatically" regarded to be experts; persons with no or only short experience were regarded as non-experts. Admittedly, often experience is needed for attaining a high performance level. However, expertise does not necessarily follow from a long experience. Therefore, at the conceptual level it is important to distinguish between expertise (i.e. high and excellent performance) and experience. The possible positive relationship between expertise and experience should rather be a topic on the agenda for empirical research than an assertion that is taken for granted.

In order to explain high performance, many expertise studies adopt a process perspective. They examine how high performers accomplish tasks, which strategies they use and on which competencies they build in the work process.

RESEARCH FINDINGS

Compared to the huge amount of studies, in which experienced individuals were compared with less experienced, research on differences between high and moderate performers is still relatively small in size. However, research findings look promising. Empirical studies in various domains show that high and moderate performers differ in the way they approach their tasks. High performers pursue more specific goals (Hershey, Walsh, Read, & Chulef, 1990) and put more emphasis on analysing the task or the problem to be solved than do moderate performers (Klemp & McClelland, 1986; Vessey, 1986). High performers aim at a good internal representation of the problem early in the work process (Klein & Hoffman, 1993). Furthermore, there is some evidence that high performers spend more time on planning (Earley, Wojnaroski, & Prest, 1987; Klemp & McClelland, 1986). More specifically, Hacker (1986) described the use of a "planning strategy" as the core characteristic of high-performing shopfloor workers—as opposed to a "momentary strategy" shown by workers at a lower performance level.

Additionally, high and moderate performers differ with respect to feedback processing, with high performers seeking more feedback (Simmons & Lunetta, 1993; Sonnentag, in press) and being particularly interested in negative feedback that points at the necessity for improvement (Ashford & Tsui, 1991). High performers possess a more comprehensive tacit knowledge in their domain of expertise (Wagner & Stemberg, 1985). In teamwork settings, they make use of highly developed communication and cooperation skills (Curtis, Krasner, & Iscoe, 1988).

Taken together, these studies have shown that high and moderate performers approach their tasks differently. High performers use different strategies and a broader knowledge for task accomplishment. Thus, it seems to be very fruitful to extend this line of research in order to arrive at a better understanding of excellence and work-related expertise. The articles presented in this Special Issue are a further step in this direction.

RELEVANCE FOR APPLICATION PURPOSES

Reliable and transferable results of research on expertise and excellent performance are of great importance for practitioners working internally or as freelance consultants. Actually, it is one of their core tasks in organizations to ensure and promote comprehensively high performance of the whole staff in order to strive for outstanding business excellence. By doing this, work and organizational psychologists contribute to a well-known, profitable, and effective appearance of the organizations in their domains.

With respect to personnel selection, expertise research can help in selecting high-performing employees by pointing out which competencies are to be measured in the selection process. This is especially important and challenging when selecting employees for future tasks, be it in the context of high potential selection for a coming project or a new responsibility, or be it in areas with quickly emerging or changing tasks and organizational settings.

Personnel selection procedures on their own are not sufficient for ensuring high performance. Additionally, training is required and is becoming increasingly important in the ongoing change process (Hesketh, 1997). By describing work strategies of high performers, expertise research can identify and suggest training needs and necessities for other individuals. For example, high performers' approaches to task accomplishment can serve as a model in the training process.

Furthermore, expertise research might be applied to career development issues. For example, studies show that high performers do not necessarily have a long, but rather a broad and varied professional experience (Sonnentag, 1995; Voss, Greene, Post, & Penner, 1983). This finding implies that, in career planning, experience in a variety of tasks and contexts should be prioritized over a long experience in only one specific context.

CONCEPT AND CONTENT OF THIS SPECIAL ISSUE

This Special Issue combines academic and practitioners' papers: Five contributions report empirical studies on high performance (Tripoli, Schaper & Sonntag, Sonnentag, van den Berg, Valkeavaara), three contributions describe practitioners' concepts and experiences (Göbel-Kobialka, Remdisch & Dionisius, Follon). In order to encourage exchange between scientific research and practice, we asked practitioners to comment on scientific articles—and vice versa.

Angela Tripoli reports an empirical study of high performance in a technical domain. She argues that in complex, high discretion jobs, employees' ability to plan and allocate time is of crucial importance. Her analyses show that focusing on work priorities, anticipating obstacles, and developing alternative plans, as well as allocating working time in accordance with supervisors' priorities, are related to high performance. Based on these findings one might conclude that not only job-specific competencies but also "meta-competencies" such as planning and time allocation are essential parts of work-related expertise, particularly in complex and ill-structured jobs.

Niclas Schaper and Karlheinz Sonntag examined expertise at the shop-floor level—a work domain not often covered in expertise research. The authors compared high and lower performers' diagnostic trouble-shooting processes. It turned out that high performers were more efficient in finding faults, and particularly in localizing the fault area. They spent less effort on irrelevant actions or simple repetitions of previous actions. These findings are interesting because they suggest that also in shop-floor level jobs mental representations and monitoring are extremely necessary for high performance. Additionally, the authors report a pilot study in which they implemented their research findings in a training programme.

The study reported by Sabine Sonnentag deals with the question of how to measure expert performance. More specifically, she studies likeability bias in peer nominations of assumed expert performers. Her analysis shows that high performers are indeed perceived to be more likeable than moderate performers. But performance differences can not be explained by differences in likeability. This finding indicates that peer nominations can be regarded as *one* approach for measuring expertise.

Peter van den Berg and Tuija Valkeavaara do not follow the traditional "contrastive approach" (Voss, Fincher-Kiefer, Greene, & Post, 1986) of comparing high and moderate performers. Rather, they examine the relative importance of competencies for various work roles within one profession. Peter van den Berg conducted his questionnaire study in the domain of business computer science and found that knowledge of information technology, working style, and analytic ability were rated as important for most computer science tasks. Additionally, communication skills were regarded to be important for a number of tasks and roles. However, the relative importance of the competencies assessed differed considerably between various professional roles *within* business computer science. This finding suggests that also within one domain there is not one uniform pattern of required competencies that holds for all roles to be performed within this domain.

The article by Tuija Valkeavaara addresses expertise in human resource developers and shows that various work roles are characterized by both specific and overlapping competencies. For example, analytical competence seems to be important for all human resource developers. This study is a good starting point for further extending expertise research to relatively ill-structured work, such as that of human resource management professionals.

Susanne Göbel-Kobialka in her contribution on "Reaching business excellence through sound people management" explains the Siemens Nixdorf Informationssysteme AG approach of identifying and developing high potentials. She describes how to clarify a position profile, how to differentiate unit-specific management career models and how to gain an overview of all excellence-relevant personal data: knowledge, professional experience, competencies. The author explains additional features of the system such as assessment and feedback procedures, the high potentials' database and the electronic job-market open to SNI employees world-wide. Adaptation of the approach to other cultural standards is proven feasible.

In their pilot study report, Sabine Remdisch and Sabine Dionisius describe a training programme for superiors which aims at the improvement of the selection process and its accuracy. Readers will first have a brief glimpse of the high potential selection and nominating process at Opel (General Motors). The authors then reveal eight company-specific core competencies (and some of their constituting items) and show how training participants become familiarized to these and how they are made more sensitive to behaviour patterns shown by their employees.

Different ways of developing expertise at work are subject of the article by Marinus Follon. The author describes how process operators' tacit knowledge and engineers explicit knowledge can be mediated by knowledge sharing loops. This mediation makes engineers capable of capturing tacit knowledge of the operators and changing it into explicit knowledge. The author reports Knowledge Based Solutions and Most Effective Technology as value-creating results.

The commentaries provided by practitioners on academic articles and by researchers on practitioners' articles show that the authors of this Special Issue cover important and relevant topics. At the same time, commentators broaden the view, question some of the—maybe too quickly accepted—interpretations, and point to unresolved research and implementation problems.

We hope that this Special Issue stimulates discussions about expertise at work. Furthermore, we wish it to encourage future research and innovations in organizations, in order to promote excellent work performance during these challenging times.

REFERENCES

Ashford, S.J., & Tsui, S.A. (1991). Self-regulation for managerial effectiveness: The role of active feedback seeking. *Academy of Management Journal, 34,* 251–280.

Curtis, B., Krasner, H., & Iscoe, N. (1988). A field study of the software design process for large systems. *Communications of the ACM, 31,* 1268–1287.

Earley, P.C., Wojnaroski, P., & Prest, W. (1987). Task planning and energy expended: Exploration of how goals influence performance. *Journal of Applied Psychology, 72,* 107–114.

Ericsson, K.A., & Smith, J. (1991). Prospects and limits of the empirical study of expertise: An introduction. In K.A. Ericsson & J. Smith (Eds.), *Toward a general theory of expertise: Prospects and limits* (pp. 1–38). Cambridge, UK: Cambridge University Press.

Hacker, W. (1986). *Arbeitspsychologie [Work psychology].* Bern, Switzerland: Huber.

Hershey, D.A., Walsh, D.A., Read, S.J., & Chulef, A.S. (1990). The effects of expertise on financial problem solving: Evidence for goal-directed, problem-solving scripts. *Organizational Behavior and Human Decision Processes, 46,* 77–101.

Hesketh, B. (1997). Dilemmas in training for transfer and retention. *Applied Psychology: An International Review, 46,* 317–386.

Klein, G.A., & Hoffman, R.R. (1993). Seeing the invisible: Perceptual–cognitive aspects of expertise. In M. Rabinowitz (Ed.), *Cognitive science: Foundations of instruction* (pp. 203–226). Hillsdale, NJ: Lawrence Erlbaum Associates Inc.

Klemp, G.O., & McClelland, D.C. (1986). What characterizes intelligent functioning among senior managers? In R.J. Sternberg & R.K. Wagner (Eds.), *Practical intelligence: Nature and origin of competence in the everyday world* (pp. 31–50). Cambridge, UK: Cambridge University Press.

Lawler, E.E.I., & Ledford, G.E.J. (1997). New approaches to organizing: Competencies, capabilities and the decline of the bureaucratic model. In C.L. Cooper & S.E. Jackson (Eds.), *Creating tomorrow's work organizations: A handbook for future research in organizational behaviour* (pp. 231–249). Chichester, UK: Wiley.

Simmons, P.E., & Lunetta, V.N. (1993). Problem-solving behaviors during a genetics computer simulation: Beyond the expert/novice dichotomy. *Journal of Research in Science Teaching, 30,* 153–173.

Sonnentag, S. (1995). Excellent software professionals: Experience, work activities, and perceptions by peers. *Behaviour and Information Technology, 14,* 289–299.

Sonnentag, S. (in press). Expertise in professional software design: A process study. *Journal of Applied Psychology.*

Vessey, I. (1986). Expertise in debugging computer programs: An analysis of the content of verbal protocols. *IEEE Transactions on Systems, Man, and Cybernetics, 16,* 621–637.

Voss, J.F., Fincher-Kiefer, R.H., Greene, T.R., & Post, T.A. (1986). Individual differences in performance: The constructive approach to knowledge. In R.J. Sternberg (Ed.), *Advances in the psychology of human intelligence* (Vol. 3, pp. 297–134). Hillsdale, NJ: Lawrence Erlbaum Associates Inc.

Voss, J.F., Greene, T.R., Post, T.A., & Penner, B.C. (1983). Problem-solving skill in the social sciences. In G.H. Bower (Ed.), *The psychology of learning and motivation: Advances in research and theory* (Vol. 17, pp. 165–213). New York: Academic Press.

Wagner, R.K., & Sternberg, R.J. (1985). Practical intelligence in real-world pursuits: The role of tacit knowledge. *Journal of Personality and Social Psychology, 49,* 436–548.

EUROPEAN JOURNAL OF WORK AND ORGANIZATIONAL PSYCHOLOGY, 1998, 7 (4), 455–476

Planning and Allocating: Strategies for Managing Priorities in Complex Jobs

Angela M. Tripoli

University College Dublin,
Department of Business Administration, Ireland

This study is an empirical examination of the planning and allocating strategies of employees in complex work roles characterized by high discretion and multiple demands. A cross-sectional survey design was used to test the relationship between particular types of strategies and individual work performance as rated by both supervisors and peers. In a sample of technical and administrative professionals, some support was found for the benefits of two planning strategies: focusing on priorities and contingency planning. A third planning strategy, anchored planning, was associated with high performance for employees with moderate experience, but not employees with very short or very long experience. In terms of allocation strategies, holding priorities which were consistent with that of the supervisor did not aid performance, but actually allocating time in a manner consistent with the priorities of the supervisor was related to individual performance. Implications for training and motivating individuals in complex jobs are offered.

In the past two decades we have witnessed a dramatic increase in high-technology and service sector firms. Organizations such as these depend upon the flexibility and astute actions of their members to accomplish complex work in a dynamic environment. This dependence has led many organizations to allow knowledge workers and other technical and service professionals some discretion in managing their work. For the employees, the combination of job complexity and discretion creates particular challenges. For example, many of the goals which are communicated to employees in these roles are only broadly specified. Employees are often left with the responsibility of determining specific goals for themselves which link to larger organizational goals. They

---

Requests for reprints should be addressed to A.M. Tripoli, Dept. of Business Administration, University College Dublin, Belfield, Dublin 4, Ireland, Email: angela.tripoli@ucd.ie

The author is indebted to the following people for their valuable comments on earlier versions of this paper: Ray Aldag, Tom Lawrence, Jone Pearce, Lyman Porter, and Anne Tsui.

must also identify how they will achieve their goals (March & Simon, 1958). All the while, they must keep in perspective the relative priority of each objective. While this may be non-problematic in theory, actions often become uncoupled from priorities in practice, i.e. when actually managing day-to-day demands. Since all responsibilities are not equally important, high performance requires some optimization of a set of objectives. These numerous demands require employees not merely to increase their efforts, but to deploy their efforts wisely in order to achieve high performance. Wood and Bandura (1989, p. 376) noted, "in complex activities, individuals' increased effort is not translated into performance gains unless they develop effective strategies for deploying that effort productively".

In an effort to learn more about employee performance in these challenging contexts, this study addressed the broad research question: What types of work strategy are associated with high performance of individuals in complex jobs? A work strategy is defined here as an employee's approach to planning and allocating effort across goals, activities, and time periods. Specifically, the empirical study focused on the question, do high performers in these contexts have a special expertise in *planning* and *allocating* to manage a set of priorities?

A basic premise of this study is that when employees are given a degree of latitude in carrying out organizational directives, the work strategies these individuals adopt play an important role in determining job performance. To illustrate, consider two employees who have the same degree of discretion in their work roles and are both equally committed to achieving a given set of organizational goals. Despite these similarities, these individuals may differ in the priority they give to each of the goals assigned to them. As well, one employee may plan out interim goals and steps for all of his or her projects, and consider potential obstacles. The other may act first and plan only in the context of action. The two employees may also differ in the way they actually allocate their time and effort to their multiple responsibilities as they carry out their work. It is argued that such differences in the manner in which individuals prioritize their work responsibilities, plan ways to meet their objectives, and allocate their time and effort, affect their ultimate work performance. Of course, we would expect the extent of such work strategy differences, as well as their impact on performance, to vary depending on both individual and contextual factors.

Clearly, the way in which individuals approach their work is often unsystematic, rather than deliberate and rational. Still, even when work activity is not deliberately systematic, patterns in people's work approaches can be detected. The term "strategy" is used here in a manner consistent with Mintzberg's (1978) conceptualization of organization strategies—that is, it refers to both "deliberate" and "emergent" patterns of activity.

In this study, I have chosen to explore work strategies from the perspective of cognitive psychology, in particular, action theory models which view work behaviour as goal directed and guided by cognitive plans (Frese & Sabini, 1985;

Frese & Zapf, 1994). Adopting this lens, my focus is both sharpened and constrained. The study focuses exclusively on work strategies that individuals use to plan and allocate their effort. This particular conceptualization of work strategies can be useful because it directs our attention to the relatively under-explored area of self-management processes which are required of individuals in complex, semi-autonomous work. The pattern of changes in organizational work roles, in particular the increase in job discretion, necessitates the development of concepts that can adequately explain variance in work performance due to differences in how individuals get their work accomplished.

WORK STRATEGIES AND PERFORMANCE IN COMPLEX WORK ROLES

Using the theoretical frame of action theory and drawing on conceptual ideas derived from the literature on complex problem solving and metacognitive models of self-regulation and motivation, three specific planning strategies and two allocation strategies are identified and conceptually developed. Each strategy is posited to be related to individual work performance.

Planning Strategies

The three planning strategies studied here involve metacognitive processes in which work responsibilities are analysed and structured. Since the planning cognitions are linked directly to action, they might be considered "action styles" (Frese, Stewart, & Hannover, 1987, p. 1183).

Priorities Focus.   Priorities focus is defined as a work strategy characterized by a broad integrated focus on one's work priorities—both while developing cognitive plans for long-range objectives and in the midst of demands for current action. This characteristic is derived from the work of Bratman (1987) and Miller, Galanter, and Pribram (1960) on plans and intentions in human behaviour. In the context of complex work roles, one's plans must lead to a *set* of goals which typically evolve over time (Brehmer, 1992). With the added complexity that goals are multiple and dynamic, a single logical plan may be insufficient. A set of intentions regarding the attainment of one goal must be integrated with intentions toward another goal, and all of this must be re-evaluated periodically. With this in mind, the concept of priorities focus is adapted here. A work strategy with high priorities focus is characterized by a continual assessment of the importance of various demands for current action in terms of their effect on meeting priorities.

Earley, Lee, and Hanson (1990) provide empirical support for the role of priorities focus in facilitating performance. In their study, employees who used work strategies which incorporated a greater breadth of work duties and a longer time frame had higher levels of performance. A sophisticated computer simulation study (Dorner, Kreuzig, Reither, & Staudel) reported by Reither and Staudel (1985) offers additional evidence of the importance of priorities focus. The simulation placed subjects in the position of mayor of a mythical town and required them to analyse the highly complex and dynamic situation, formulate specific goals based on abstract "global" goals, set up priorities, and implement strategies. The most successful subjects (i.e. those that best achieved the global goals) prioritized aspects of the situation according to criteria essential to the global objectives; whereas the less successful subjects prioritized in terms of "the probability of success of affecting one particular aspect of the problem" (p. 114). Poorer performers were not able to work on the problem as a whole. Instead they had a tendency to focus on one particular aspect alone, or jump from one subgoal to another, which Brehmer refers to as "thematic vagabonding" (Brehmer, 1992, p. 226).

If work strategies involve attending to each goal separately, there is a greater risk for individuals to engage in activities which are not consistent with their overall priorities. Therefore, it is hypothesized that, in general:

Hypothesis 1:   The greater *the priorities focus* of a work strategy, the higher will be the employee's performance.

Anchored Planning.   A work strategy can vary in the degree to which intentions are planned out. Miller et al.'s (1960) classic work noted that plans vary in the amount of detail they include. In the context of complex work, detailed planning may not even be possible or appropriate. Brehmer (1992) argues that where all the features of the problem are not readily apparent (opaqueness) and the state of the problem changes over time (dynamic), plans may need to be preceded by some initial testing of hypotheses. This is also supported by Isenberg's (1988) study of senior managers. In this study, the focus moves away from sheer level of detail. The focus is on the extent to which the employee's planning process specifies goals, activities, and time frames. This concept, labelled *anchored planning*, refers not to any particular plan of action, but rather to the *process* of planning itself. It is the cognitive process of working through the breakdown of projects into interim goals, actions to take, and time frames. Thus, anchored planning is conceptualized here as having three dimensions: goals, actions, and time anchoring.

Recent action theory research seems to support the benefits of planning in general. By delineating plans, an individual creates a path to accomplish goals (Frese & Sabini, 1985; Frese & Zapf, 1994). In the context of complex work, the anchored planning process can uncover useful information to move forward regardless of whether any final plan can be executed as is. Thus the anchored planning process can serve as a cognitive guide for action.

As well as providing a cognitive guide for action, anchored planning may also improve performance by enhancing individual motivation. Goal setting theory argues that specified goals operate as a cognitive mechanism to motivate and improve performance (Locke & Latham, 1990; Locke, Shaw, Saari, & Latham 1981). Yet, in a dynamic, unstructured work context, employees must meet goals that tend to be high level objectives (e.g. finish a research paper, develop a contract proposal), rather than the "specific" goals prescribed by goal-setting theory. Employees' efforts to decompose the high-level goals and define more precise performance criteria in the form of several partial goals become increasingly critical for success on the job. Subgoals create concrete criteria for an individual to use in assessing whether he or she is making progress toward a goal (Kanfer & Ackerman, 1989; Reither & Staudel, 1985). Therefore, some anchoring in terms of setting operational goals should help to improve performance.

In addition to specifying goals, specifying actions and time frames to achieve one's goals may also improve performance. An individual may strongly desire to achieve a goal and may value the rewards associated with the achievement of the goal; yet, if he or she cannot determine the means that will allow him or her to accomplish the project, motivation and progress will flounder (Earley, Connolly, & Ekegren, 1989; Earley, Connolly, & Lee, 1989; Earley & Perry, 1987; Heckhausen & Kuhl, 1985; Vroom, 1964). Through anchored planning, a diffuse desire to perform well becomes translated into sequences of subgoals and specific action needed to satisfy that desire. The worker moves from a state of passive "want" to active intention and finally into action (Heckhausen & Kuhl, 1985). Thus, anchored planning may provide self-motivation.

Results of the Dorner et al. (cited in Reither & Staudel, 1985) computer simulation experiment support the assertion that more effective planning strategies are specified on goal, activity, and time dimensions. More successful subjects were more apt to develop hierarchical plans by iteratively establishing goals, going into action planning, then returning to the "superordinate" goal level again (Reither & Staudel, 1985, p. 115). Sonnentag (in press) conducted a field study of software designers and found that high performers carried out more "local planning" in which they articulated their next step. Yet the high performing designers did not engage in more "planning ahead" than did moderate performers. However, Sonnentag suggests that the nature of software design may make planning ahead less important, since subtasks need not be finished in a fixed sequence. This problem feature differs from that faced by many managerial and administrative professionals. Finally, Frese, Stewart, and Hannover's (1987) study of "planfulness" in an educational setting found no significant relationship between planfulness and performance as measured by grade point average.

In summary, the cited studies provide mixed theoretical and empirical support for the relationship between anchored planning and performance; however, most of the empirical work has been mainly experimental studies or looking at non-work contexts. It seems reasonable to assume that the relationship between anchored planning and performance would depend on the both the nature of the work and the organization. It is posited that in work contexts characterized by complexity, yet with some degree of rationality and predictability, anchored planning will be positively associated with work performance.

Hypothesis 2a: The greater the *anchored planning* of a work strategy, the higher will be the employee's performance.

However, highly detailed and coordinated strategies may still not lead to effective performance if they are inappropriate to the problem at hand. When planning, time which could be invested directly into action is invested in the cognitive construction of future action. The challenge is to ensure that the investment tradeoff results in more appropriate actions. Therefore, a simple relationship between planning and performance may be difficult to predict.

If work experience is factored in, the relationship may be more clear. Work experience can provide an individual with the practical knowledge necessary to determine the best tactic to take for a given work project. Earley et al. (1990) found that individuals with more experience adopted better "quality strategies", that is, strategies which were more appropriate to the situation. It is posited that more experienced individuals are better able to judge how long each step will take and how feasible each activity and subgoal is. Thus, the following hypothesis is offered.

Hypothesis 2b: The relationship of *anchored planning* to work performance will be stronger for those employees with higher levels of relevant work experience.

Contingency Planning.   Individuals can also incorporate *contingency planning* into their work strategies. This characteristic of work strategies involves the anticipation of potential events and the consideration of alternative plans. Individuals vary in the extent to which they consider contingencies which may pose obstacles while they are attempting to carry out their plans, and they differ in the degree to which they overtly incorporate viable options in developing their plans. Contingency planning need not—and most often does not—involve a full articulation of several hierarchical paths to a single goal. Rather, it can be characterized as the metacognitive process of working through a series of possible events and reasonable alternative plans.

Anticipating potential obstacles and considering alternative plans reduces an employee's dependence on being able to implement any one plan. Contingency planning may allow the employee to still capitalize on preplanning if unexpected contingencies block the pursuit of any one linear plan (Bratman, 1987). In the Earley et al. (1990) study, employees noted that contingency planning was one aspect of their overall work plans that they found useful in achieving their work goals. Frese et al. (1987) included contingency planning as one aspect in their operationalization of "planfulness". Their study of a student sample provided somewhat contradictory evidence: "Planfulness" and grade point average were not significantly related. More evidence on the performance benefits of contingency planning needs to be done in work organization contexts. Therefore, the following hypothesis is posited:

Hypothesis 3:   The greater the extent of *contingency planning* of a work strategy, the higher will be the employee's performance.

Allocation Strategies

The challenge of managing multiple demands in a complex job also means effectively allocating attention and time across a set of responsibilities. With numerous demands, one must be able to determine the most important ones and allocate effort accordingly. The implications for effective work strategies is that they cannot be designed and carried out in isolation. What constitutes effective performance for an employee is dependent on the expectations held by others in the organization (Tsui, 1984). An individual may have engaged in integrated, anchored, and adaptive planning, but this is unlikely to be sufficient to result in effective performance if the employee's work priorities and time allocation are widely disparate from those prescribed by others in his or her role set. The term "allocation strategies" is used here to refer to the ways in which employees assign differential priority and time to the various tasks and responsibilities assigned to them. In organizations, a critical issue seems to be whether an employee's prioritization and time allocation are in agreement with that of others who may rate his or her performance.

Prioritization Fit.   The level of agreement between an employee and his or her supervisor or peers on work role priorities is referred to as *prioritization fit.* Tsui (1984) found that ratings of a manager's effectiveness by different constituencies were positively related to the degree to which the manager met the constituencies' expectations. This suggests that evaluations of an individual's performance reflect the evaluator's priorities, which may not necessarily be consistent with those of the individual. Thus, to some degree, employee performance is a function of prioritization fit. The following hypothesis is offered.

Hypothesis 4:   The greater the *prioritization fit* of a work strategy, the higher will be the employee's performance.

Time Allocation Fit.   Even when employees' priorities are ostensibly consistent with those of the organization, employees may find that in the face of day-to-day demands their actual actions reflect different priorities than those they intended. For example, a faculty member at a university may place a higher value on research than teaching and therefore cognitively rank research higher in priority. In actually carrying out work activity each day, the same person may allocate more time to teaching than to research. Thus, actual time allocation seems to reflect different priorities than those espoused by the individual.

In this study, the objective was to look not merely at perceptions of role priorities, but also priorities in action, i.e. the manner in which employees actually allocate their time across a set of responsibilities. Especially when faced with multiple demands and limited time, employees must meet the challenge of not only intending, but actually allocating their time in a manner consistent with the priorities of the person evaluating them. Agreement between an employee's time allocation across responsibilities and the prioritization of those responsibilities by the supervisor or peers is referred to here as *time allocation fit*.

Hypothesis 5:   The greater the *time allocation fit* of a work strategy, the higher will be the employee's performance.

METHODS

The hypotheses were tested using a cross-sectional survey design. The data collection was designed to minimize common source variance.

Sample

The participants for this study were technical and administrative professionals employed in an information systems branch of a large provincial ministry on the west coast of Canada. Employees in work roles with multiple work responsibilities and moderate to high discretion were selected in order to maximize the observed variability on work strategy characteristics. To identify employees with at least moderate work role discretion, Breaugh's Work Autonomy Scales (Breaugh & Becker, 1987) were included in the study questionnaires. Two subscales of the instrument measure discretion regarding procedures used in carrying out work and discretion concerning timing and sequencing of activities. Employees who scored an average of 3.5 or greater on a seven-point scale were judged to have adequate work role discretion. The median age of participants was between 36 and 45 years. Twenty-two per cent were women. The average tenure with the organization was just over 16 years, and years of education ranged from 11 to 20 years.

Procedures

All potential participants were given survey packets including full instructions. A total of 85 focal surveys were sent out; 68 were returned, giving a response rate of 80%. Of these, 66 who met the criterion of at least moderate work role discretion were included in the study.

Following the return of the focal surveys, peer and supervisor surveys were distributed to collect performance and prioritization data on the focal participants. The peers for each focal participant were selected on the basis of their interdependence with the focal employee. This criterion was used to ensure that peers had some familiarity with the focal employee's work. Focal employees listed several co-workers with whom they worked closely. The research officer within the organization verified the work interdependence of each peer listed. Then, from the remaining list, two co-workers were randomly selected by the researcher. A total of 126 peer surveys were distributed; 80 were returned, giving a peer response rate of 63%. Twenty-five supervisors were sent surveys. Completed surveys were returned from 16 supervisors, providing data on 50 focal employees, giving a response rate of 64%.

All participants were assured of confidentiality. Surveys were identified only by code numbers. Questionnaires were completed independently and mailed directly to the researcher.

Scale Development and Pilot Testing

Measures for the work strategy characteristics and work performance were developed specifically for this study since existing measures on related concepts were not similar enough in content domain or were context-specific. An initial set of items for each construct was derived from the relevant literature. Some items were dropped or modified based on two rounds of pilot testing, including preliminary interviews with six individuals in high discretion work roles and pilot surveys administered to 40 university faculty, and engineers and marketing specialists employed in an electronics firm. All pilot participants were independent of the main study sample. Procedures and standards outlined by Nunnally (1978) and Carmines and Zeller (1978) were followed in determining the composition of the final scales to be used for the study measures.

Measures

Priorities Focus.   Priorities focus, operationalized as a clear and broad focus on one's work priorities, was measured with a six-item scale with a coefficient alpha 0.78. A sample item was: "I regularly review my priorities before determining what task/project to work on next." A seven-point agree-disagree response scale was used.

Anchored Planning. The measure for anchored planning included items related to each of the three dimensions of the construct: goal, activity, and time considerations. Sample items included: "When I sit down to work on a project, I usually set some sort of *goal* which I must accomplish for that period of work"; "For the various projects on which I am working, I usually plan out the *action steps* that I intend to take"; "I usually develop *timetables* for most of the projects on which I am working." The same seven-point agree-disagree response scale was used. The coefficient alpha for the scale was 0.88. A principal components analysis with varimax rotation conducted on the entire set of 13 items resulted in a three-factor solution, reflecting the three dimensions. Given that the internal consistency measure was sufficiently high and the conceptual aim was to sample the breadth of the construct's domain, all of the items were retained in the final scale.

Contingency Planning. Contingency planning was defined as an individual's tendency to anticipate potential obstacles and alternative plans when carrying out work. The six-item measure had a coefficient alpha of 0.87 and a single-factor solution in a principal components analysis. A sample item was: "I usually like to consider more than one approach to accomplishing a project, in case one approach does not work well." Again, the seven-point agree-disagree response scale was used.

Prioritization Fit. To obtain a measure of the fit between the employee's prioritization of responsibilities and that of the supervisor, a list of responsibilities was developed and included in the survey. This list was developed through an iterative process. First, an initial list of responsibilities was generated by the research officer of the organization. Then, during a series of meetings with the officer and through review by five employees in the organization, the list was modified to ensure meaningful categories and terminology. On the survey, focal employees were asked to rank their responsibilities in order of the priority they gave each one in their work. Supervisors and peers were asked to rank the responsibilities in order of the priority they believed each should be given in the focal individual's work. This allowed comparisons to be made between focal employees' and supervisors' (or peers') priorities. The priority ranks for each of the top five priorities as identified by the supervisor (or peer) were compared with the ranks given to those responsibilities by the focal employee. The absolute value of the difference scores was calculated for these top priorities. Because a difference on the highest priority of the performance evaluator may be more serious than a difference on the fifth priority, the difference scores were weighted accordingly (i.e. evaluator's ranking of the priority [reverse-scored] × difference score [reverse-scored]). The difference score was also reverse-scored so that a high score reflected a better fit.

Time Allocation Fit. On the survey, employees also reported the percentage of their work time that they spent on each of their responsibilities. The time allocation fit score was obtained by calculating the percentage of time allocated by the focal individual to the responsibilities rated as the five highest priorities by the supervisor (or peer).

Work Experience. A measure of "total related work experience" was obtained by summing the responses of two items: (1) "Number of years/months in this job in this current organization," and (2) "Number of years/months in a similar position in another organization."

Performance. Performance ratings were obtained from the focal individual's supervisor and up to two co-workers. This avoided the problem of common source variance in testing the hypotheses, and allowed for comparisons of reports from two constituencies. The "performance" scale included five items which asked the rater to assess the focal individual's performance in terms of how effectively and efficiently he or she met the major objectives of his or her work role over the course of the preceding year. Sample items included: "Effectiveness in accomplishing the major objectives of his or her job"; "Effectiveness in meeting deadlines and completing projects in a timely manner". The coefficients alpha for the performance scale were 0.92 for peers and 0.95 for supervisors. The zero-order correlations between the supervisor and peer ratings was 0.33 ($P < .01$) and the correlations between the two peer raters was 0.25 ($P < .05$). Although the relationships were significant, their relatively low value suggests that performance evaluators used somewhat different criteria and perceptions in judging performance. This is a pervasive challenge in trying to measure performance, both in organizations and in research. In an attempt to deal with this problem, control variables were included in all of the regression analyses.

Control Variables.   The theoretical arguments posited here have focused on the performance-facilitating capacity of work strategies. Yet, the measure of performance used in this study (and in most organizations) is not an objective assessment of accomplishment. Performance ratings are made by peers and supervisors whose perceptions may be influenced by a number of factors unrelated to accomplishment and productivity. One such factor is "interpersonal attraction". Two items were included: (1) "How well to you like working with this individual?" Responses were rated on a five-point Likert-type scale ranging from "not at all" to "to a very great extent"; and (2) "How often do you socialize with this individual outside of work?" The correlation between the two items was low ($r = 0.11$) and Cronbach's alpha was 0.20. Therefore, summing the standardized items was not deemed appropriate. However, since both items could potentially influence performance ratings, both (i.e. "working relationship" and "time spent socializing") were included as separate controls in the analyses for testing the hypotheses.

Validity Check. A 10-item version of the Marlow-Crowne "social desirability" scale (Strahan & Gerbasi, 1972), MC 1(10), was included as a validity check on the work strategy scales. One concern with self-report methodology is that respondents are merely providing "socially desirable" answers to the questions. As one check on this validity concern, scores on each of the work strategy planning characteristics were correlated with scores on the social desirability scale. No significant relationships were found.

RESULTS

Table 1 presents the intercorrelation matrix of all study variables. To test each of the hypotheses, two sets of analyses were run. First, a model which included all performance raters (peers and supervisors) tested the incremental variance explained by each strategy after controlling for the effects of "working relationship" and "time spent socializing". This model was run using each focal-rater dyad as a case. Second, separate analyses were run using only peer performance data and then using only supervisor data.

Tables 2 and 3 report the results of the hierarchical regression models used to test Hypotheses 1, 2a, and 3 which state that the planning strategies will be significantly related to employees' performance ratings by peers and supervisors. In the first model, which includes all raters, *priorities focus* and *contingency planning* accounted for a significant amount of variance in performance ratings, after controlling for the interpersonal attraction variables. *Anchored planning* did not predict performance. When the peer and supervisor models were run separately, the pattern of results was similar. Using peer ratings of performance, *priorities focus* and *contingency planning* accounted for some variance, although the significance level was low ($P < .10$). Again *anchored planning* did not account for a significant amount of variance. Using supervisor ratings, only *priorities focus* accounted for variance in performance ($P < .10$).

In each of these models, the addition of the block of work strategy variables resulted in a significant change in R^2. Thus, the overall results provide some support for a positive relationship between two planning strategies and performance: *priorities focus* and *contingency planning*.

The argument in Hypothesis 2b was that some basic level of work experience is needed to capitalize on anchored planning. This suggests that after some length of work experience, the effect of anchored planning on performance becomes stronger. To test the hypothesized relationship, the sample was split into three equal groups using frequencies on employees' years of work experience. The cut-offs were ≤ 5 years (low experience), 6–20 years (medium experience), and 21–40 years (high experience). From this an interaction term was created, first by trichotomizing the experience variable, then multiplying this by anchored planning. To test the interaction effect, first hierarchical regressions were run, including the control variables, the main effects for work experience and anchored planning, and the interaction term. The interaction term was significant for the model which included all raters of performance ($\beta = .54$, $t = 3.12$, $P < .01$) and for the model using only peer ratings ($\beta = .63$, $t = 3.12$, $P < .01$). The changes in R^2 were 0.06 ($P < .01$) and 0.09 ($P < .01$) respectively. The interaction was not significant when using supervisor ratings ($\beta = .41$, $t = 1.36$, $P = .18$); however, the degrees of freedom were too low to make a meaningful interpretation of those results.

In order to further understand the interaction found, regressions were run for each subsample (i.e. low, medium, and high work experience) to test the relationship between anchored planning and work performance at the three levels of experience. The control variables were included in each regression. Due to the small sample size, separate analyses for peers and supervisors could not be run. For the group with low work experience, anchored planning accounted for a small amount of variance in performance ($\beta = .25$, $t = 1.91$, $P < .10$). For the group with a medium level of experience, anchored planning was more strongly related to performance ($\beta = .31$, $t = 2.11$, $P < .05$). Finally, for those with high experience, anchored planning had no effect on performance ($\beta = -.01$, $t = -.09$, $P = .93$). Overall, these results indicate that some form of interaction exists between anchored planning and work experience, although the relationship with performance appears to be more complicated than hypothesized.

Hypothesis 4 posited that employee performance would be rated more highly if the employee's prioritization of responsibilities was consistent with that of the person rating performance. This was not supported by the results of the regression analyses. As shown in Table 4 *prioritization fit* was not significantly related to employee performance, as rated by peers or supervisors.

Finally, Hypothesis 5 was supported. In the model including all peers' and, supervisors' performance ratings, *time allocation fit* was significantly related to performance ($\beta = .35$, $t = 2.86$, $P < .01$), even after controlling for *prioritization fit*. When comparing the separate peer and supervisor models, it appears that time allocation fit accounted for a significant amount of performance variance as rated by supervisors ($\beta = .41$, $t = 2.45$, $P < .05$) but accounted for less variance in performance as rated by peers ($\beta = .34$, $t = 1.70$, $P = .10$).

DISCUSSION

The results of this study provide some evidence to support the hypothesized relationships between several types of work strategies and work performance among the professionals in the sampled context. Employees who reported higher levels of the planning strategies, *priorities focus* and *contingency planning*, received significantly higher performance ratings by their supervisors and peers than did those reporting lower levels. Thus, the direct relationships between work strategy planning characteristics and performance were supported with the notable exception of *anchored planning*. While the simple relationship between anchored planning and performance received little support, an interaction between *anchored planning* and work experience was supported.

TABLE 1
Means, Standard Deviations, and Intercorrelations of Study Measures

	N	Mean	SD	1	2	3	4	5	6	7	8	9	10	11
1. Anchored planning	63	4.64	0.86	1.0										
2. Contingency planning	65	5.31	0.85	0.66***	1.0									
3. Priority focus	66	4.88	0.82	0.54***	0.5***	1.0								
4. Priority fit (with peers)	26	244.5	51.2	−0.01	−0.26	0.19	1.0							
5. Priority fit (with supervisors)	27	232.3	47.0	0.09	−0.14	−0.12	0.71**	1.0						
6. Priority fit (with all raters)	53	238.3	49.0	0.04	−0.21	0.04	1.0	1.0	1.0					
7. Time allocation (with peers)	61	47.9	24.6	−0.20	−0.25*	0.12	0.16	−0.15	0.16	1.0				
8. Time allocation (with supervisors)	35	50.7	20.9	−0.13	0.06	0.15	0.05	−0.19	−0.19	0.87***	1.0			
9. Time allocation (with all raters)	101	49.0	23.4	−0.18	−0.15	0.12	0.16	−0.19	0.0	1.0	1.0	1.0		
10. Working relationship (with peers)	81	4.12	0.91	−0.33**	−0.10	−0.09	−0.03	0.35	−0.03	0.12	0.04	0.12	1.0	
11. Working relationship (with supervisors)	48	4.02	0.98	−0.07	−0.07	−0.10	−0.14	−0.14	−0.14	0.12	0.0	0.0	0.31*	1.0
12. Working relationship (with all raters)	129	4.09	0.94	−0.23*	−0.09	−0.09	−0.03	−0.14	−0.09	0.12	0.0	0.0	1.0	1.0
13. Experience	64	13.0	10.7	−0.13	0.01	−0.01	0.08	−0.04	0.0	0.14	−0.08	0.07	0.06	−0.16
14. Time socializing (with peers)	81	0.73	3.21	−0.17	−0.12	−0.10	−0.38	−0.29	−0.38	0.09	0.11	0.09	0.10	0.18
15. Time socializing (with supervisors)	48	0.40	0.79	−0.02	−0.13	−0.07	−0.23	0.03	0.03	0.10	−0.02	−0.02	0.12	0.26
16. Time socializing (with all raters)	129	0.60	2.59	−0.13	−0.11	−0.12	−0.38	0.03	0.14	0.09	−0.02	−0.04	0.10	0.26
17. Social desirability	64	5.77	1.93	0.19	−0.02	−0.03	0.24	0.13	0.24	−0.04	0.01	−0.04	−0.03	0.11
18. Work role discretion	66	5.42	0.86	0.16	0.25*	0.20	0.16	−0.05	0.06	0.30*	0.38*	0.32***	0.0	0.0
19. Performance (rated by peers)	81	3.33	0.85	0.0	0.20	0.21	−0.19	−0.16	−0.19	0.27*	0.52***	0.27*	0.44***	0.0
20. Performance (rated by supervisors)	48	3.57	0.96	0.23	0.29*	0.36**	−0.26	−0.12	−0.12	0.32*	0.34*	0.34*	0.04	0.35*
21. Performance (rated by all raters)	129	3.42	0.90	0.1	0.25**	0.26**	−0.19	−0.12	−0.17	0.27*	0.34*	0.29**	0.44***	0.35*

	12	13	14	15	16	17	18	19	20	2
12. Working relationship (with all raters)	1.0									
13. Experience	-0.03	1.0								
14. Time socializing (with peers)	0.10	-0.09	1.0							
15. Time socializing (with supervisors)	0.26	0.16	-0.03	1.0						
16. Time socializing (with all raters)	0.11	-0.06	1.0	1.0	1.0					
17. Social desirability	-0.03	0.12	0.17	0.14	0.17	1.0				
18. Work role discretion	0.0	-0.07	-0.20	0.16	-0.13	0.11	1.0			
19. Performance (rated by peers)	0.44***	-0.04	-0.09	-0.03	-0.09	-0.27	0.11	1.0		
20. Performance (rated by supervisors)	0.35*	0.0	-0.03	0.41	0.41**	-0.06	0.34*	0.33**	1.0	
21. Performance (rated by all raters)	0.39***	-0.11	-0.09	0.41	-0.02	-0.27	0.21	1.0	1.0	1.0

*P < .05; **P < .01; ***P < .001.

TABLE 2
Hierarchical Regression Analyses of Performance Ratings on Planning Strategies—Overall Model

	Performance	
	Rated by Peers and Supervisors	
	β	t
Control variables (entered as a block)		
Working relationship	.38	4.87***
Time spent socializing	.26	3.33**
Work strategy characteristics (entered as a block)		
Anchored planning	−.13	−1.14
Contingency planning	.25	2.24*
Priorities focus	.27	2.93**
ΔR^2	·14***	
Overall model R^2	.37	
Adjusted R^2	.34	
Overall model F	13.42***	
N	121	
Degree of freedom	5, 115	

*$P < .05$; **$P < .01$; ***$P < .001$.

TABLE 3
Hierarchical Regression Analyses of Performance Ratings on Planning Strategies—Individual Models

	Performance			
	Rated by Peers		Rated by Supervisors	
	β	t	β	t
Control variables (entered as a block)				
Working relationship	.44	4.08****	.33	2.58**
Time spent socializing	.12	1.14	.36	3.82**
Work strategy characteristics (entered as a block)				
Anchored planning	−.16	−1.02	−.05	−.30
Contingency planning	.26	1.75*	.20	1.04
Priorities focus	.23	1.92*	.30	1.95*
ΔR^2	.11*		.19**	
Overall model R^2	.34		.65	
Adjusted R^2	.29		.42	
Overall model F	7.06****		5.85****	
N	74		46	
Degrees of freedom	5, 68		5, 40	

*$P < .10$; **$P < .05$; ***$P < .01$; ****$P < .001$.

470

TABLE 4
Hierarchical Regression Analyses of Performance Ratings on Allocation Characteristics—Overall Model

	Performance	
	Rated by Peers and Supervisors	
	β	t
Control variables (entered as a block)		
Working relationship	.17	1.35
Time spent socializing	.29	2.31*
Work strategy characteristics (entered as a block)		
Prioritization fit	−.11	−.92
Time allocation fit	.35	2.86**
ΔR^2	·13*	
Overall model R^2	.29	
Adjusted R^2	.23	
Overall model F	4.81**	
N	53	
Degree of freedom	4, 48	

$*P < .05; **P < 0.1.$

TABLE 5
Hierarchical Regression Analyses of Performance Ratings on Allocation Characteristics—Individual Models

	Performance			
	Rated by Peers		Rated by Supervisors	
	β	t	β	t
Control variables (entered as a block)				
Working relationship	−.04	−.20	.33	1.90*
Time spent socializing	.17	.75	.33	1.93*
Work strategy characteristics (entered as a block)				
Prioritization Fit	−.18	−.84	−.01	−.05
Time allocation fit	.34	1.70[a]	.41	2.46**
ΔR^2	.12		.17*	
Overall model R^2	.19		.40	
Adjusted R^2	.03		.30	
Overall model F	1.22		3.73***	
N	26		27	
Degrees of freedom	4, 21		4, 22	

$[a]P = .10; *P < .10; **P < .05; ***P < .001.$

Employees with moderate levels of work experience were able to gain more performance benefits from investing in anchored planning. However, employees with less than five years experience also gained some small benefits. The difference between the two groups may be due to the novice employees' lack of accurate information and poor estimations which make time spent in planning less useful. An interesting and unexpected finding was that employees with very long experience did not improve their performance with anchored planning. One explanation is that with such extensive experience, planning becomes less explicit (Sonnentag, 1996). Yet, a one-way ANOVA revealed no significant differences in the means for anchored planning among the three levels of experience. Another possible interpretation is that after a significant length of time in the same type of job, we become fixated on particular strategies and do not necessarily adapt them to new situations. Isenberg (1988) argued that we tend to apply old assumptions to novel situations. In his study of successful senior managers, he found that they were able to pay attention to "feelings of surprise" and then highlight the novelty of the situation (p. 535). Sonnentag (1996) found that length of experience did not predict either knowledge about useful strategies or the actual application of these strategies. Thus, there may be a liability of experience operating, wherein too much experience in the same type of job may inhibit an employee from formulating appropriate plans in new situations.

The relative effect of each of the characteristics is indeterminate as yet. In general though, planning which specifies goal, activity, and time dimensions appears to play a role in work effectiveness for employees with moderate experience. Yet, contingency planning may play an even stronger role in general. This highlights the need for both proactiveness and flexibility in managing one's work. Priorities focus appeared to be the work strategy planning characteristic most strongly related to performance. The important role of this variable is consistent with previous studies conducted by Dorner et al. (cited in Reither and Staudel, 1985), in which prioritization was found to result in better performance on a decision-making simulation.

The results related to the allocation strategies were particularly interesting. Agreement between employees and supervisors on espoused priorities was not related to employee performance. Yet, agreement on actual time allocation did predict performance. It seems that for employees, holding appropriate priorities is not enough to ensure high performance ratings. It appears to be more important to actually allocate one's time in a manner consistent with supervisor priorities. This suggests a practical distinction between "priorities in theory" and "priorities in use." High performers may indeed have an expertise in allocating effort in a manner consistent with the important demands in the work environment. Furthermore, the low zero-order correlation (0.12) between *time allocation fit* and *priorities focus* suggests that allocation expertise requires more than a cognitive focus on priorities.

A study of this type poses several challenging validity issues. In particular, the introduction of new measures presents construct validity concerns.[1] The cognitive nature of the work strategies examined in this study necessitated a self-report methodology which introduced a potential self-report bias. To avoid the common source variance problems associated with self-report, performance data were collected from sources other than the focal participants. This approach, coupled with low, non-significant correlations found between the self-reported levels of work strategies and the social desirability measure, provides some confidence that the empirical relationships between strategies and performance are not merely a function of self-report bias.

One methodological concern, however, is the issue of asking individuals to report on their work strategies when those strategies may be largely un-conscious—especially for employees with a great deal of work experience. Experience tends to transform conscious action plans into scripts. However, other theorists studying the phenomenon of plans and intentions (e.g. Tubbs & Ekeberg, 1991) have argued that although scripted behaviour is carried out largely unconsciously, individuals can be made aware of the action plans they are following. In other words, even though we typically go about our work with little meta-thought regarding the particular approaches we are using, when called upon to do so, we can articulate those approaches. Still, it would be useful to supplement self-report cognitive data with additional methods such as observation, especially for the non-cognitive concepts such as "time allocation".

An alternative explanation for the strength of some of the relationships is that work strategies and performance may be causally linked in the opposite direction to that conceptualized. This argument may have some merit for the interpretation of the relationship between performance ratings and priorities focus in particular. High performers may rationalize that because they have performed well, they must have carefully considered their priorities on a regular basis. Low performers on the other hand, would experience more cognitive dissonance in indicating that they engaged in consistent clarification of their priorities and yet still did not perform well. Thus, reported levels of priorities focus may be influenced by the individual's perceived performance. Given this concern with self-report bias, additional measures of priorities focus in particular are warranted.

The small sample size in this study limited the types of analyses that could be performed. In particular, it would have been useful to test a full model, including all work strategy and control variables, to identify relative effects more clearly. With the small sample size, the reliability and generalizability of the results are restricted.

---

[1]Please contact the author for the results of tests for discriminant and convergent validity of the work strategy measures. These were omitted here due to limited space.

CONCLUSIONS AND IMPLICATIONS

For organizations facing dynamic environments and accomplishing work of a complex nature, a part of the organizational technology may reside in the minds of the workers. In turn, work is being structured by employees themselves, rather than solely by management. The results of this study suggest that the high performers in complex jobs with multiple demands are those who structure their work by keeping a broad and coherent focus on priorities. They are able to keep this view of the big picture while building in flexibility through planning for contingencies. With some experience, individuals in these jobs may also benefit from anchored planning. Along with these cognitive planning strategies, high performers are able to prioritize their time across multiple demands in a way that reflects the priorities of their management.

The planning strategies studied here require time, information, and analysis to develop. Descriptive research on how people actually plan their work and allocate their time indicates that many individuals dislike and tend to avoid the analysis and specification involved in planning (e.g. Mintzberg, 1973; Reither & Staudel, 1985; Sonnentag, 1996). Yet the results of this study suggest that certain types of planning may improve work performance. This poses a distinct challenge in managing employees in complex work roles. This challenge is reflected in the study by Sonnentag (1996) who found that with particular work experience (e.g. high amount of design work) software designers may gain more knowledge about useful work strategies, yet they will not necessarily use these strategies. Furthermore, as noted earlier, she found that *length* of experience alone did not predict either knowledge about useful strategies or the actual application of these strategies.

Taken together, these findings suggest some important implications for human resource management. First, planning strategies can benefit performance, yet work experience in and of itself is not enough to provide employees with knowledge of effective planning and allocating strategies. Therefore, training programmes should focus on explicit development of such skills. Second, to motivate employees in complex work roles, we may need to focus more on what factors inhibit and encourage the use of metacognitive processes such as planning and prioritizing. Individuals in complex work roles have both the opportunity and the necessity to influence their cognitions and motivation through the ways in which they structure their work. Finally, the stronger role of time allocation fit over prioritization fit indicates that communication and clarification between supervisors and employees regarding work priorities is not enough to ensure that employees manage multiple demands optimally. Attention needs to be paid to creating a bridge between intentions and actions. Again, more training should focus on the skill of following through on intentions and maintaining one's priorities in a dynamic environment.

REFERENCES

Bratman, M.E. (1987). *Intention, plans, and practical reason.* Cambridge, MA: Harvard University Press.

Breaugh, J.A., & Becker, A.S. (1987). Further examination of the work autonomy scales: Three studies. *Human Relations, 40,* 381–400.

Brehmer, B. (1992). Dynamic decision making: Human control of complex systems. *Acta Psychologica, 81,* 211–241.

Carmines, E.G., & Zeller, R.A. (1978). *Reliability and validity assessment.* Beverly Hills, CA: Sage Publications.

Earley, P.C., Connolly, T., & Ekegren, G. (1989). Goals, strategy development, and task performance: Some limits on the efficacy of goal setting. *Journal of Applied Psycholology, 74,* 24–33.

Earley, P.C., Connolly, T., & Lee, C. (1989). Task strategy interventions in goal setting: The importance of search in strategy development. *Journal of Management, 15,* 589–602.

Earley, P.C., Lee, C., & Hanson, L.A. (1990). Joint moderating effects of job experience and task component complexity: Relationships among goal setting, task strategies, and performance. *Journal of Organizational Behavior, 11,* 3–15.

Earley, P.C., & Perry, B.C. (1987). Work plan availability and performance: An assessment of task strategy priming on subsequent task completion. *Organizational Behavior and Human Decision Processes, 39,* 279–302.

Frese, M., & Sabini, J. (Eds) (1985). *Goal directed behavior: The concept of action in psychology.* Hillsdale, NJ: Lawrence Erlbaum Associates Inc.

Frese, M., Stewart, J., & Hannover, B. (1987). Goal orientation and planfulness: Action styles as personality concepts. *Journal of Personality and Social Psychology, 52,* 1182–1194.

Frese, M., & Zapf, D. (1994). Action as the core of work psychology: A German approach. In H.C. Triandis, M.D. Dunnette, & L.M. Hough (Eds), *Handbook of industrial and organizational psychology, Vol. 4.* Palo Alto, CA: Consulting Psychologists Press.

Heckhausen, H., & Kuhl, J. (1985). From wishes to action: The dead ends and short cuts on the long way to action. In M. Frese & J. Sabini (Eds), *Goal directed behavior: The concept of action in psychology.* Hillsdale, NJ: Lawrence Erlbaum Associates.

Isenberg, D.J. (1988). How senior managers think. In D. Bell, H. Raiffa, & A. Tversky (Eds), *Decision making: Descriptive, normative, and prescriptive interactions.* Cambridge, UK: Cambridge University Press.

Kanfer, R., & Ackerman, P.L. (1989). Motivation and cognitive abilities: An integrative/ aptitude-treatment interaction approach to skill acquisition. *Journal of Applied Psychology, 74,* 657–690.

Locke, E., & Latham, G. (1990). *A theory of goal task performance.* Englewood Cliffs, NJ: Prentice Hall.

Locke, E., Shaw, K., Saari, L., & Latham, G. (1981). Goal setting and task performance, 1969–1980. *Psychological Bulletin, 90,* 125–152.

March, J.G., & Simon, H.A. (1958). *Organizations.* New York: John Wiley & Sons.

Miller, G.A., Galanter, E., & Pribram, K.H. (1960). *Plans and the structure of behavior.* Holt, Rinehart & Winston.

Mintzberg, H. (1973). *The nature of managerial work.* Harper & Row.

Mintzberg, H. (1978). Patterns in strategy formation. *Management Science, 24,* 934–948.

Nunnally, J.C. (1 978). *Psychometric theory.* New York: McGraw-Hill.

Reither, F., & Staudel, T. (1985). Thinking and action. In M. Frese & J. Sabini (Eds), *Goal directed behavior: The concept of action in psychology.* Hillsdale, NJ: Lawrence Erlbaum Associates Inc.

Sonnentag, S. (1996). Planning and knowledge about strategies: Their relationship to work characteristics in software design. *Behaviour and Information Technology, 15*, 213–225.

Sonnentag, S. (in press). Expertise in professional software design: A process study. *Journal of Applied Psychology.*

Strahan, R., & Gerbasi, K.C. (1972). Short, homogeneous versions of the Marlow-Crowne Social Desirability Scale. *Journal of Clinical Psychology, 28*, 191–193.

Tsui, A.S. (1984). A role set analysis of managerial reputation. *Organizational Behavior and Human Performance, 34*, 64–96.

Tubbs, M.E., & Ekeberg, S.E. (1991). The role of intentions in work motivation: Implications for goal-setting theory and research. *Academy of Management Review, 16*, 180–199.

Vroom, V. (1964). *Work and motivation.* New York: Wiley.

Wood, R.E., & Bandura, A. (1989). Social cognitive theory of organizational management. *Academy of Management* Review, *14*, 361–384

A Commentary on "Planning and Allocating: Strategies for Managing Priorities in Complex Jobs" by A.M. Tripoli

Jürgen Deller, Daimler Benz Inter Services (debis) AG, Berlin, Germany

Individuals in complex job environments are successful when they concentrate on priorities, think of risks and plan their time according to management priorities. The mere knowledge of these priorities is not sufficient in order to show high performance evaluated as such by managers and peers but of course is a condition *sine qua non* to plan time accordingly. It is remarkable that these decisive factors of work performance are not in the main focus of consideration of human resources management, neither in selection nor development.

But can the presented results be transferred to other samples or populations? Or do we have to consider these results to be probably business or job specific, maybe also culture dependent? Can the results of this study be transferred to different job families characterized by similarly complex and only poorly predefined work routines also to jobs in Europe? Are—for our European demands—probably different strategies promising? As an example I would like to discuss the question: What defines the orientation to priorities? Following the item presented by the author, priorities seem at least partially to be defined by the task *per se.* In order to work successfully in a team, factors besides pure task orientation are critical to success. At least doubts could arise, with a team of purely task-oriented members, doubts concerning the cohesion and successful cooperation of this team.

Let's say the results can be transferred. In this case questions need to be raised concerning the selection of team members: Can different strategies of successful work behaviour be measured besides using self assessment? And if so, are these rather general abilities to develop adequate work strategies or is it really possible to train them to a high degree? What would be appropriate training designs? This is a question for moderating variables. What is the reason that beginners and very experienced individuals profit only a little from anchored planning? What exactly must novice employees be trained in to let them benefit from the advantages of anchored planning? And: What can individuals with little or moderate job experience learn from successful individuals with high experience since in this case anchored planning seems again to be counter productive? Together with Tripoli we have to seek the moderating factors that encourage the use of meta-cognitive processes such as planning and prioritizing. The answers to these and further questions will enable us to design effective training measures for specific personnel development.

Last but not least such new results must be reflected in the framework of personnel politics, in the way a company is managed. In debis, a step in this direction is a pay agreement on service-specific work conditions, for example on the guarantee of openness concerning work time management.

Tripoli's work showed interesting results that shed a new light on the construction of human resource management tools. Answers to the questions raised are essential to use the results effectively.

EUROPEAN JOURNAL OF WORK AND ORGANIZATIONAL PSYCHOLOGY, 1998, 7 (4), 479–498

Analysis and Training of Diagnostic Expertise in Complex Technical Domains

Niclas Schaper and Karlheinz Sonntag

*Psychological Institute, University of Heidelberg,
Germany*

In the following report, two studies on analysis and training of expert performance in troubleshooting at complex manufacturing plants will be presented. The first and main study deals with a comparison of experts and novices to assess the level of expertise necessary to complete complex diagnostic tasks. Critical behavioural elements and cognitive processes of high performing maintenance technicians were identified by observing maintenance technicians with different levels of expertise while troubleshooting real faults. In addition, training needs were derived from the assessment of inefficient and deficient performance of low performing technicians. The particular training needs emerged in narrowing down the faults and in generating an adequate mental representation of the fault conditions. These findings are discussed with respect to current research in this domain.

In the second study, a training programme designed to improve on the exchange of knowledge between experts and novices was evaluated. In this training programme, the acquisition of information search and information processing strategies were taught through elements of the cognitive apprenticeship approach. In addition, mapping techniques were used in group discussions to facilitate the development of knowledge structures that support problem solving in troubleshooting. A first training evaluation shows that diagnostic performance can be improved through this approach.

INTRODUCTION

Expertise is needed to competently perform tasks that are characterized by a great multitude and complexity of requirements and by a great variety and uncertainty of situational patterns (Gruber & Ziegler, 1996). In order to identify the specific abilities and/or learning processes which represent expert

Requests for reprints should be addressed to N. Schaper, Psychological Institute, University of Heidelberg, Hauptstrasse 47–51, D-69117 Heidelberg, Germany.

We are grateful to Sabine Sonnentag and two anonymous reviewers for important hints to improve a former version of the article and to Susanne Brauer and Kimberley Feldt who helped us to compose a readable English version of the article.

performance, com-parisons are conducted between experts and novices. The results of such comparisons can be used to identify training needs. They can serve two purposes in this context. First, this method leads to a profound insight into the properties of expert performance in terms of cognitive processes and knowledge structures. This helps to define what should be taught and which are the training goals. Second, the observed differences in cognitive processes or knowledge structures can be interpreted as deficient action components of the low performing group. This information can be used to get a close and concrete picture of the performance status of the training group and to select relevant training contents.

The analysis of expert performance to determine training needs is based on a specific concept of expertise. Such an analysis focuses on persons who possess highly effective action regulation structures for a specific task or domain. Training in complex tasks aims at acquiring expert knowledge and abilities. An expert is classified by his or her high and excellent performance in a domain and the comparison of novices and experts is based on criteria of performance and not on criteria of job experience. The latter are not valid indicators for outstanding or high vocational performance, as shown in a number of studies (Hacker, 1992; Sonnentag, 1995).

After a survey of the current research on expertise addressing technical diagnostic tasks, an expertise study in an authentic task context is presented here. In this study, the training needs of maintenance technicians were analysed by means of an expert–novice comparison. Then the design and evaluation of a training approach is described based on cooperative exchange of knowledge between experts and novices.

RESEARCH IN EXPERTISE OF TECHNICAL DIAGNOSIS

In industry, and in everyday use, technical systems are disrupted or malfunction, which makes it inevitable to have the system tested or repaired by professional technicians. Specific requirements are necessary to efficiently identify the causes of the malfunctions and to eliminate the fault (Sonntag & Schaper, 1997). Due to the following reasons, the diagnosis of the malfunction or the search for the cause can be often particularly difficult and is associated with problem solving requirements:

- Technical troubleshooting tasks require a broad and detailed knowledge of the system and potential malfunctions (Rasmussen, 1986; Schaper, 1995).
- The multitude of faults is usually not immediately perceptible, nor accessible, without additional aids (Bereiter & Miller, 1989; Schaper & Sonntag, 1995).

- The strategies for narrowing down and identifying the faults are complex; algorithms can rarely be applied to them (Konradt, 1992; Rasmussen, 1986).

With regard to these high cognitive demands in technical diagnosis, it seemed appropriate to apply the perspective of expertise research to this domain. Accordingly, the relevant questions are: Which prerequisites for effective performance are characteristic for persons that efficiently master these complex and difficult types of tasks, and how are these prerequisites acquired? Research in expertise has already addressed diagnostic judgement (Krems, 1994), but these studies have mainly focused on tasks in medical diagnoses. Additional studies have dealt with debugging computer programs (Krems, 1994; Vessey, 1986), and with cognitive processes of diagnostic judgement analysed in abstract or artificial contexts on the basis of a general psychological perspective (Hoc & Amalberti, 1995). A considerable range of research has already been conducted on the topic of troubleshooting in technical systems. Expert–novice comparisons, however, are rarely applied in this context.

According to Krems (1994), the process of diagnostic judgement can be divided into three sub-processes or components. Each of these components have been investigated with regard to differences between successful and less success-ful problem solvers: (1) Problem identification and representation: Within this subcomponent, important cognitive processes include the analysis of initial conditions of the diagnostic problem and focusing the attention on fault relevant parts of the technical system. (2) Generation of hypotheses and information search: In this subprocess, a sample of potential malfunctions is selected that is relevant to guide the subsequent strategy in problem solving. (3) Diagnostic procedures and problem solving strategies: This component refers to the selection of appropriate operations for finding a successful and efficient solution to the diagnostic problem.

Problem Identification and Representation. According to Greeno and Simon (1988), the superiority of expert performance is due to abilities associated with problem representation. It has been shown repeatedly, that experts perceive a task in terms of essential features, i.e. they identify immediately the principle or the underlying rules of the task (e.g. Chi, Feltovich, & Glaser, 1981). Consequently, they are capable of distinguishing important from unimportant aspects in problem solving. Novices, on the other hand, tend to rely on superficial features of the task and, as a consequence, they develop a representation of the problem that is inefficient for the subsequent information processing. Patel and Groen (1991) studied the cognitive processes of problem representation in medical domains with physicians. Their findings, however, do not support the results of Chi et al. (1981). In the context of medical diagnostic tasks, different levels of expertise cannot, be clearly classified with regard to problem representation. In the context of technical diagnostic tasks, however, Wiedemann (1995) was able to provide evidence for the assumption presented earlier. This author observed apprentices, advanced trainees, and skilled maintenance technicians in troubleshooting at an electropneumatic bending device and analysed differences in the amount of successful diagnoses, in the required time of diagnosis, and the total number of diagnostic actions. The results showed that experienced maintenance technicians utilize a strategy which is supported by relevant hypotheses, whereas apprentices tend to pay more attention to superficial properties of the device.

Generation of Hypotheses and Information Search.   In medical domains, differences in hypothesis generation and information search based on competence and experience are discussed with reference to two approaches. The first is based on the work of Elstein, Shulman, and Sprafka (1978) who found evidence for deductive strategies. The second was developed by Patel and her colleagues (e.g. Patel & Groen, 1991) who interpreted their observations in terms of an inductive strategy. The deductive strategy is characterized by an early generation of hypotheses that guide the subsequent information search. In contrast, the diagnostician who uses an inductive strategy is guided by case-specific information and develops and refines his or her hypotheses concurrently. In order to successfully perform this "data-driven", "forward" strategy of information processing, broad and detailed knowledge based on experience is required. According to Patel and Groen (1991), the deductive, "backward" procedure, where the information processing evolves from hypotheses, is mostly observed in novices or unexperienced diagnosticians. Regarding research on these processes in technical domains the following studies should be mentioned: Mehle (1982) analysed the process of hypothesis generation when identifying faults in defective motor vehicles. The author confronted his subjects with an unspecified damage of a motor vehicle and asked for hypotheses about possible causes of this damage. Additionally, the subjects had to rate their level of certainty regarding their hypotheses. Mehle (1982) found that novices and experts did not differ in the number of generated hypotheses or their degree of certainty. Krems and Bachmaier (1991) investigated diagnostic behaviour of apprentices, skilled workers and foremen in motor mechanic workshops. They instructed their subjects to generate hypotheses over an unspecified damage of a motor vehicle. In the second part of the study, the fault-finding processes in three motor vehicle defects were simulated by a card technique. By requesting cards, the subjects could access further diagnostic information until the cause of the fault could be identified. In contrast to results obtained in other diagnostic domains (Johnson, Hassebrock, Duran, & Moller, 1982), experts in motor vehicle defects tested fewer and more specific hypotheses even in a more limited search space than novices did. Instead of a "breadth-first" strategy of information search with unspecific hypotheses, experts prefer a "depth-first" search that includes quite specific hypotheses even in the initial stages. They are also capable of substituting false assumptions with correct alternative hypotheses in a flexible way. Due to their experience and knowledge, experts have immediate access to further possible fault categories. So, unlike novices, experts do not retain their false hypotheses very long.

Diagnostic Procedures and Problem-solving Strategies.   Differences in the strategic repertoire or strategic procedures between experts and novices were mainly investigated according to their specificity (global vs. specific) and to their direction (forward vs. backward). With increasing experience, the specificity of the strategic repertoire improves. Beginners tend to adopt global strategies that are not domain specific, termed "weak" methods, whereas experts use domain-specific "strong" methods (Joseph & Patel, 1986). Similar findings were reported by Konradt (1992), who elicited retrospective descriptions of troubleshooting faults in CNC (computerized numerical control) machine tools through semi-structured interviews. The verbal protocols were subsequently analysed according to 16 strategy categories of content analysis. Depending on job experience, Konradt (1992) discovered that experts mention a greater number of strategies than novices, i.e. they possess a broader repertoire of strategies. Additionally, experts prefer strategies that rely on experience and those emerging from direct sensoric perception. In contrast, novices tend to use strategies that reflect on high probability faults or fault possibilities that are easily tested. Furthermore, they prefer strategies that refer to manuals of the line. Konradt (1992) also provides evidence that beginners prefer "backward" or goal-oriented strategies whereas experts tend to use "forward" or data-driven procedures. Further analyses of Konradt's interview data showed that novices exhibit "topographic" diagnostic strategies, whereas experts additionally use "symptomatic" and "case-based" strategies. The first two categories refer to Rasmussen's (1986) distinction between "topographic" and "symptomatic" strategies. Using topographic strategies, the structure and signal flow of the system are taken into account by the troubleshooter. So, paths are identified to test the functioning of line modules and components. This strategy corresponds to the goal-oriented or "backward" strategy. Symptomatic strategies are characterized by processes that involve the detection and classification of malfunction patterns according to defined classes of different malfunction causes. That corresponds to data-driven "forward" strategies.

In summary, it can be concluded that experts in technical diagnosis differ from novices in the following aspects: Experts avoid diagnostic steps in their information search that are concerned with the global status of the technical system, which can be interpreted as a "forward" or "data-driven" strategy. This strategy implies, also, a generation of hypotheses based upon a relatively small amount of data. False assumptions made by experts, however, do not lead to severe mistakes or disadvantages, because experts are capable of substituting false hypotheses early with correct alternatives. Furthermore, we can conclude from the analyses of diagnostic procedures and strategies, that experts use different strategies to novices in troubleshooting. Experts prefer symptomatic and case-based strategies, which rely on experience and direct sensoric information. Novices use methods that are not so knowledge dependent and are more easy to execute.

Most of the presented studies are based on verbal reports or behavioural analyses that were investigated in the context of abstract or artificial tasks. A transfer of these findings to the real job context has to be discussed critically: Verbal reports only reflect parts of expert competence. Aspects that are automated or cannot be verbalized, but that are nevertheless relevant for regulation, are not recognized. The application of knowledge and abilities can be very different depending on the context (Perkins & Solomon, 1989). Under abstract or artificial conditions, genuine behaviour and the whole breadth of knowledge might not be exhibited. Therefore, the described features of troubleshooting experts have to be tested on their validity in real life tasks.

TROUBLESHOOTING PERFORMANCE OF EXPERTS AND NOVICES IN FLEXIBLE MANUFACTURING SYSTEMS

Questions of Research

The following study was part of a larger research programme aimed at the analysis of training needs for diagnostic tasks in flexible manufacturing systems. In the preceding steps, the conditions and requirements of maintenance jobs were analysed and described by means of different job and task analyses (Schaper & Sonntag, 1995). The specific focus of this study was the comparison of competent troubleshooters with inexperienced and low performing problem solvers in order to identify critical elements of troubleshooting behaviour in such contexts. Based on this goal, the following research questions were formulated: In what respect do competent troubleshooters differ from inexperienced or low performing problem solvers? Which conclusions can be drawn from this analysis concerning type and quality of action regulation and which training needs for the low performing population can be derived?

Design and Method of the Expert–Novice Comparison

In an automobile production plant, a total of 19 maintenance technicians were observed while diagnosing two electrical faults on a welding transfer line. On the transfer line, car body shells were tacked and welded in several steps. Automatic transfer devices interlinked 16 work stations that were each equipped with one welding robot. The transfer line was controlled by a logic programmable control (LPC). In addition, each work station had a local robot control. Under normal conditions, the line was run by two operators. To create standardized observational conditions and tasks for the quasi-experimental comparison, faults of the line were simulated. Thus, each of the maintenance technicians involved in the study was confronted with the same malfunctions. These were selected according to different levels of complexity. The first line trouble—of medium complexity—comprised a defective relay contact in the signal course of the start prerequisites. The second line trouble was more complex and consisted of a defective output of a valve control in the signal course of a gripping device. (In the following section, the words "fault", "malfunction", "line trouble" will be used as synonyms).

After the faults had been installed into the system, the subjects were individually called to the line and instructed to find the fault. They were provided with the same sources of information and equipment as those used in normal troubleshooting tasks (e.g. computer assisted diagnostic aids, an LPC device that provides information about the structure and state of the LPC program, and the hardware and software plans of the line). A line operator was also available to answer questions about the system status or how to operate the line. During the troubleshooting process, the maintenance technicians were observed by a research assistant and an instructor. The research assistant recorded each information request and each testing action in sequential order according to a coding system that had been developed for this study. He also recorded verbal descriptions and explanations of the subjects' activities. We refrained from instructing the subjects to think aloud as the use of tape recorders was not possible. The maintenance technicians were allowed 30 minutes to find each malfunction. After finishing the first diagnostic task, the testing was briefly interrupted in order to install the second malfunction. Then, the subject was again introduced to the malfunction by an operator. If the maintenance technician reached a "dead end" in his search (i.e. if he did not know how to continue), he was provided with minimal assistance, so that each subject could proceed and was observed in all sequences of the diagnostic process. In order to analyse the cognitions that regulate activities, retrospective interviews were conducted after the subjects had performed both tasks. The subjects were asked to recapitulate their strategy in the course of diagnosis and to depict their assumptions and conclusions concerning the malfunction. At the end of the interview, they were asked about their vocational education, job experience, and job domain. The interviews were taped and transcribed.

In order to assess the level of expertise of each subject, the diagnostic behaviour shown while handling both tasks was rated by an instructor of the maintenance technicians. This instructor can be considered a "super-expert" because he possessed very high troubleshooting skills and technical knowledge.

He also had trained the participating technicians and had supervised them in various practical problems. The subjects were rated according to the following scales: (1) level of systematic proceeding (1 = very systematic, 2 = systematic, 3 = partially systematic, 4 = unsystematic, 5 = very unsystematic); (2) efficiency of procedure (1 = very efficient/with low expenditure, 2 = efficient, 3 = partially efficient, 4 = inefficient/complicated, 5 = very inefficient/with high expenditure). The instructor rated the subjects independently from the researcher's observations and protocols. Five subjects were parallelly rated by a second trainer/ foreman. The interrater-consistency was $r = 0.78$ (Spearman's Rho). As both trainers had only casual opportunities to observe the subjects' diagnostic skills in the everyday work context, we refrained from assessing a rating of the overall diagnostic competence. Based on these ratings, the whole group was divided into two subgroups: one of high performing maintenance technicians, 7 subjects with high (1 and 2) ratings; and one group of low-performing maintenance technicians, 12 subjects with medium (3) and low (4 and 5) ratings. The contrastive comparison of the performance that will be presented in this article is based on this classification.

Sample

Nineteen maintenance technicians took part in the study. Each of them had been educated as an industrial electrician or was just about to finish his apprenticeship. Their job experience varied from 2 months to 14 years. The high performing technicians showed an average job experience of 8.7 ($SD = 4.5$) years, whereas the low performing technicians had only 2.1 ($SD = 2.8$) years of experience. Concerning the job domain, the whole sample worked in one maintenance section of the production plant and they all specialized on electrical faults of the line.

Content Analysis

The records of the observations and interviews were analysed by means of a content analysis according to Mayring (1988). Using this technique, the verbal data were analysed according to a theoretical structure. This structure was applied to the data as a categorical system in order to extract systematically all aspects of the text that represent these categories. Quantitative analysis procedures were applied to the extracted structure in subsequent steps.

The study dealt with strategic behaviour in troubleshooting. These strategies were to be examined according to different characteristics. The following main and subcategories were developed for the investigation.

Diagnostic Actions

This category referred to the type and number of actions a maintenance technician performs. Each action referred to a single diagnostic step, which was executed to obtain information about the condition of the system. Diagnostic actions were for example "conducting a single volt measurement", "testing a system function by pressing a button", or "requesting fault messages at the control panel". A low number of diagnostic actions was interpreted as a measure for efficiency. This is in accordance with studies (e.g. Hennemann & Rouse, 1984) where the number of diagnostic operations was found to be negatively correlated with other coefficients related to the efficiency of the diagnostic problem solving.

Sequences of the Diagnostic Process

Based on antecedent rational task analysis, the diagnostic process was divided into five distinct sequences.[1] These sequences marked sections of the diagnostic problem-solving process, where definite subgoals are to be reached. Consequently, each sequence consisted of several different diagnostic actions. The ideal diagnostic procedure in each sequence was based on different strategic principles that referred to Konradt's (1992) categories. The sequences were defined as follows.

Identification of System Status ("strategy of reconstruction" according to Konradt, 1992). In this sequence, an operator obtained information about history and actual status of the line malfunction by interviewing the operator.

Localizing the Fault Area ("program diagnosis"). The analytic actions that were performed in this sequence are necessary to narrow down the search to the disrupted functions of the line subsequently called "fault area". This was mainly done by the use of technical diagnosis programs.

Splitting (identical to Konradt, 1992). This category referred to diagnostic actions that restrict the subsequent search to the hardware or software response input or output of the PLC.

Searching by Manuals and Exploration of the Fault Area ("document-based search"). This sequence contained actions enabling the technician to orientate himself about the structure and state of hardware components relating to the potential fault area. This orientation was supported by hardware plans.

---

[1]The model of Krems (1994) concerning three components of the process of diagnostic judgement was not considered useful to analyse diagnostic sequences in this context. Though these components might also be interpreted as sequences in the diagnostic process, they cannot be separated from each other with regard to their occurrence on the time dimension. They are better understood as parallel subprocesses which determine the progress of the diagnostic problem solving.

Signal Tracing ("tracing of signal courses").   This is the final sequence in the diagnostic process. By circuit measurements and by testing the functions at the actual fault area, the malfunctioning component was detected and identified step by step.

Analysing the sequences of the diagnostic process, conclusions about the strategic behaviour of maintenance technicians can be drawn. The observed frequency of identical sequences can serve as a cue for interruptions and changes in the strategic behaviour. The range of the diagnostic sequences, measured by the number of actions in each sequence, provides information on how efficiently the particular sequence was mastered.

Hypotheses

As assumptions about potential causes of faults, hypotheses regulate action during the diagnosis of malfunctions depending on their specificity and correctness. The hypotheses that were reported during the retrospective interview were, therefore, evaluated whether it had been a "correct" or "false" hypothesis and whether it had been formulated in "global" or "specific" terms. The correctness and specificity of the hypotheses was rated independently by two analysts. If the ratings diverged, they were discussed until an agreement was reached.

Deficient Diagnostic Actions

In assessing learning requirements in diagnostic behaviour, it was also important to analyse faulty or erroneous diagnostic actions. These actions included the following.

- *Irrelevant Actions*, i.e. actions that did not lead to the acquisition of useful diagnostic information concerning the potential fault area (e.g. testing the functions of irrelevant system components).
- *Repeated actions*, i.e. actions that had already been performed during the diagnostic process at least two or more times.
- *Assisted actions*, i.e. errors in performance, that corrupted the progress in the detection of the fault so that help by an instructor is required (e.g. forgetting to close the protective shutter before checking system functions in the single step mode).

In a partial probation, the categorical system that has been described here was tested for objectivity (Cohen's "Kappa"). The following results were obtained for the different classes of categories: diagnostic actions ($K = 0.95$), sequences of the diagnostic process ($K = 0.83$), hypotheses ($K = 0.91$), deficient diagnostic actions ($K = 0.70$). These measures refer to the rater agreement of the subcategories of each class of categories.

Results of the Expert–Novice Comparison

Total Number of Diagnostic Actions.   The number of observed diagnostic actions was analysed separately for each malfunction. Table 1 presents the average number of actions that were required by high and low performers in order to detect the faults. The results showed that high performers need significantly less diagnostic actions for both diagnostic tasks. Thus, competent troubleshooters proceed with greater efficiency. This leads to the question: Which features of expert behaviour accounted for this result? Due to limited space, only data of the second fault will be presented here. The data of the first fault show analogue results (Schaper, 1995). Job experience only weakly contributed to the explanation of the differences in the number of diagnostic actions. The correlation of both scores (Spearman) were quite low and not significant (defective relay contact $r = 0.22$; defective valve control $r = 0.08$).

Number of Actions per Sequence of the Diagnostic Process.   In a subsequent step, the number of observed actions were analysed for each sequence of the diagnostic process. Based on this analysis, it was possible to evaluate how efficiently the sequences have been performed and which of the sequences were characterized by specific differences in performance. The results (see Table 1) showed a significant difference concerning two of the sequences: "localizing the fault area" and "searching by manuals or exploration of the fault area". These differences were especially high at "localizing the fault area". Thus, low performers showed problems in efficiently using the diagnostic aids of the control panel and the programming device in order to narrow down the area where the fault lies. More detailed qualitative analysis of the diagnostic actions and the retrospective interviews revealed that the information search of low performers during this sequence could be characterized as global and not goal based. Within this sequence, low performers, for example, requested information from the control panel that was irrelevant for the detection of the malfunction or that served to examine the program structure of the LPC rather than for fault finding. Furthermore, in the retrospective interview, this group often mentioned very global and rather inefficient heuristics concerning this sequence (e.g. "I always check all of the diagnostic aids at the control panel before I find something").

Frequency of Identical Sequences in the Diagnostic Process.   Interruptions and changes of strategies in the course of the diagnostic search were analysed by looking at the frequency of identical sequences (see Table 1). Again, differences were found concerning localizing the fault area and in the manual-based search or the exploration of the fault area. Due to the small frequencies though, these differences were not significant. Nevertheless, it is important to note that competent troubleshooters performed each sequence only once or twice, while

TABLE 1
Diagnostic Actions and Sequences of High and Low Performers

	Groups		Mann-Whitney Test	
	High Performers	Low Performers	U	P
Number of diagnostic actions for different faults:				
Defective relay contact				
M	13.4	23.8	11.0	.01**
SD	5.1	9.5		
Defective valve-control				
M	16.7	30.3	16.5	.01**
SD	7.4	9.7		
Number of actions for each diagnostic sequence (defective valve-control):				
Identifying the system status				
M	1.0	1.5	28.0	n.s.
SD	0.0	0.8		
Localizing the fault area				
M	5.3	15.3	12.0	.01*
SD	3.6	10.8		
Splitting				
M	2.0	1.8	36.5	n.s.
SD	2.0	1.9		
Searching by manuals				
M	2.4	4.8	19.0	.04**
SD	1.0	3.2		
Signal tracing				
M	6.0	6.9	21.5	n.s.
SD	7.6	3.3		
Frequency of identical diagnostic sequences (defective valve-control):				
Identifying the system status				
M	1.0	1.2	31.0	n.s.
SD	0.0	0.2		
Localizing the fault area				
M	1.3	2.6	21.0	n.s.
SD	0.5	1.5		
Splitting				
M	0.6	0.6	55.0	n.s.
SD	0.3	0.4		
Searching by manuals				
M	1.4	2.4	22.0	n.s.
SD	0.7	1.3		
Signal tracing				
M	1.4	2.0	26.0	n.s.
SD	0.5	0.7		
Repetitions of diagnostic sequences				
M	1.5	4.6	17.0	.03*
SD	0.6	0.9		

*P < .05, **P < .01, n.s. = not significant.

low performers tended to repeat the sequences two or more times. These "repetitions" were summed up for all sequences and the comparison of this variable showed a significant difference for the two expertise groups. The repetition of sequences were interpreted as indicators for unsystematic strategic proceeding, i.e. the diagnostic actions within the sequences were not executed consequently and/or the subject changed arbitrarily between different strategies.

Number and Quality of the Hypotheses Generated in the Diagnostic Process.   In order to achieve insight into the cognitive processes regulating action in a trouble-shooting context, the hypotheses that were recorded in the retrospective interviews were analysed for number, correctness, and detail. Table 2 shows that low performers had a tendency to generate more diagnostic hypotheses though this difference was not significant. Furthermore, the number of false hypotheses is small for this group and did not deviate from the respective number of competent troubleshooters. Also, the test of the differences between the groups concerning the correctness of the hypotheses was not significant. Even the assumption that low performers should generate a higher number of global hypotheses could not be verified.

Number and Type of Deficient Diagnostic Actions.   In a final step, the frequencies of different types of deficient diagnostic action were analysed. Table 2 shows that the diagnostic behaviour of low performers was characterized to a considerably greater extent by deficient actions than that of competent troubleshooters. This held true for the total number and for the three different types of deficient actions, too. Large differences were also found for repeated diagnostic actions, a finding that hints at an insufficient analysis during the information search and during the testing actions. Due to incomplete or faulty information processing, low performers had to repeat diagnostic actions several times. But even competent troubleshooters showed deficient diagnostic actions, though to a much smaller extent.

Number of Deficient Actions with Regard to Type of Diagnostic Action.   As was shown in Table 2, deficient actions were found mostly in requests at the control panel and requests regarding program status. This fact supported our finding that low performers only inefficiently localized the fault area. Both behavioural categories were crucial in this diagnostic sequence.

Discussion of Results and Training Needs

The comparison of high and low performing troubleshooters showed that considerable differences in performance existed between the two groups. Those were interpreted in terms of inefficient or deficient action regulation which have to be improved by qualification or job design. We discuss the results in

TABLE 2
Diagnostic Hypotheses and Deficient Actions of High and Low Performers

	Groups		Mann-Whitney Test	
	High Performers	*Low Performers*	*U*	*P*
Number of diagnostic actions for different faults:				
Total number of hypotheses				
M	3.1	4.6	20.5	n.s.
SD	1.7	2.7		
Correct hypotheses				
M	3.0	4.3	28.0	n.s.
SD	1.8	2.4		
False hypotheses				
M	0.2	0.5	40.5	n.s.
SD	0.3	1.6		
Global hypotheses				
M	1.0	1.6	33.5	n.s.
SD	1.4	2.3		
Specific hypotheses				
M	2.1	3.0	32.0	n.s.
SD	3.0	2.8		
Frequency of different types of deficient actions (defective valve-control):				
Total number of deficient actions				
M	2.4	12.0	10.5	.01**
SD	1.1	5.4		
Irrelevant actions				
M	0.9	3.9	18.5	.04*
SD	1.2	3.9		
Repeated actions				
M	0.9	5.5	17.0	.04*
SD	1.2	6.3		
Assisted actions				
M	0.7	2.6	13.5	.02*
SD	0.8	1.9		
Number and kind of deficient diagnostic actions (defective valve-control):				
Requests at the control panel				
M	0.9	3.0	19.5	.05*
SD	0.3	1.2		
Requests regarding program status				
M	0.6	4.1	12.5	.02*
SD	0.5	1.7		
Volt measurement				
M	0.0	0.9	23.0	n.s.
SD	0.0	0.2		
Function test in single step mode				
M	0.3	0.9	29.5	n.s.
SD	0.5	0.4		
Visual checks				
M	0.0	0.3	37.0	n.s.
SD	0.0	0.4		
Reading of the hardware plan				
M	0.0	0.3	38.0	n.s.
SD	0.0	0.4		

*$P < .05$, **$P < .01$, n.s. = not significant.

accordance to the classification of the process of diagnostic judgement into three subcomponents by Krems (1994).

Concerning problem identification and representation, we found evidence that the generation of mental models is insufficient during these sequences. Low performing technicians showed difficulties in generating an adequate mental representation of the malfunction. This can be concluded from the high number of repeated and irrelevant diagnostic actions. Only when incorrect or insufficient analyses of information had been conducted during the antecedent operations, then repeated interrogation of the system became necessary. These observations are in accordance with the findings of Wiedemann (1995). His reconstructions of searching paths showed that inexperienced and low performing troubleshooters repeatedly tested device components in close relation to the actual fault, but they did not recognize important diagnostic cues when testing these components. The author concluded that this can be due to an insufficient mental model or from deficient hypothesis generation in the troubleshooting process.

Regarding generation of hypotheses, we found that high performers generated only slightly fewer hypotheses and that they did not differ in correctness and detailedness of hypotheses from the low performers. This partially corresponds to the results of Krems and Bachmaier (1991), as well as Mehle (1982), referring to the number and correctness of hypotheses. Contrary to Krems and Bachmaier (1991), high performers did not generate more specific or less global hypotheses. Due to the small number of hypotheses, however, differences might be hard to detect. Furthermore, this result can be influenced by the method of recording. Retrospective rehearsals of cognitive processes are fallible to the omission of mistakes, repetitions, and uncertainties that occurred during the problem-solving process (Cuny, 1979).

Concerning the use of diagnostic procedures and problem-solving strategies, the described results were interpreted in the following way. Differences in performance mostly occurred in the diagnostic sequence of localizing the fault area and the manual-oriented search or exploration of the fault area. By analysing the frequency of identical diagnostic sequences, the results revealed that these sequences were particularly problematic for the low performing subjects. Due to unsystematic strategies, low performers had to return several times to certain sequences. So, it can be concluded that inefficient strategies or a lack of heuristics for the acquisition and analysis of information within these sequences were responsible for these results. It was reported that low performing troubleshooters often search for information in a very global and not goal-oriented manner when they try to narrow down the fault area. Accordingly, novices mentioned very global and inefficient heuristics in the information search process. Krems and Bachmaier (1991) also found that novices were significantly more concerned with global diagnostic information. The authors interpreted this as a "breadth-first" strategy in information search. Our behaviour analysis in a real life context showed that this was a quite inefficient strategy due to the high number of diagnostic actions in localizing the fault area.

The following training needs can be derived from the described comparison of experts and novices regarding two subcomponents: (1) Problem identification and representation: Low performers have to be supported and instructed how to develop adequate mental models of typical or potential malfunctions. These aids and instructions should closely refer to real malfunctions that can occur at the lines of the maintenance technicians' job domain. (2) Diagnostic procedure and problem solving: Further need for training exists regarding the strategic behaviour during the sequence of localizing the fault area. Low performers should be instructed and introduced to heuristics for efficiently narrowing down the fault area. We assume that specific procedures are more efficient than the training of global principles. The transfer of global strategies into real situations requires considerably greater cognitive resources by the maintenance technician.

Training Diagnostic Expertise

In an additional study, a diagnosis training programme was designed and evaluated that is supposed to support the development of diagnostic expertise. Contrary to training approaches that favour the use of simulations (e.g. Lajoie & Lesgold, 1992), or fixed training units in courses (e.g. Patrick, 1993), our approach emphasized a continuous learning process on the job. The training was designed in accordance with "constructivistic" approaches, which are especially dedicated to the training of strategic knowledge for complex tasks in authentic or real life situations (Duffy, Lowyck, & Jonassen, 1993). Furthermore, these approaches are based on the assumption that expertise in most cases depends to a great extent on situated cognitions and experience (Law & Wong, 1996). Therefore, effective strategies and mental models can best be developed in the context of application and by systematic reflection and analysis of authentic learning experiences.

The *cognitive apprenticeship* is an instructional approach that pays attention to "constructivistic" design principles (e.g. "Use of authentic and situated learning task", "Use of multiple contexts and multiple perspectives in learning", or "Learning in a social context"). It focuses on the teaching of knowledge and strategies by experts (Collins, Brown, & Newman 1989). This approach combines principles and features of the traditional craftsman education system with elements of cognitive training. It aims at teaching complex problem solving in job domains with high cognitive demands. Not only does the problem solver have to demonstrate how to proceed in solving a task, but he also has to explicate the strategies and the underlying mental operations he uses. We utilized this approach in teaching diagnostic strategies through experts directly at the line. First, the experienced technicians were told to solve the line troubles co-operatively, that means, in cooperation with a low performing technician. While troubleshooting, the maintenance technician explained and justified his actions. Subsequently, the event had to be described in detail on a documentation sheet that had been developed for the training, including status of malfunction, cause(s), testing action(s), repair action(s). Then the novice was told to review what the expert technician actually did. Difficult or particularly critical sequences were discussed in detail and alternative solutions were considered. In subsequent troubleshooting events, the novice technician was supposed to detect and remove the fault on his own. The experienced technician provided help if necessary and supported the independent troubleshooting.

In addition to verbal and observational learning, *mapping techniques* are recommended because they allow for the visualization and structuring of knowledge, particularly for complex domains and procedural structures (Jonassen, Beissner, & Yacci, 1993). Mapping techniques represent knowledge structures by networks of knots (which represent concepts, e.g. persons, objects, incidents) and edges (which represent relations between concepts, e.g. "is part of", "is the cause of"). The use of mapping techniques in vocational learning supports:

- active elaboration and (re-)construction of knowledge
- mental rehearsal/probing of actions in complex tasks or problem situations
- flexible use of knowledge
- communication about knowledge
- cooperative knowledge acquisition and problem solving (Schaper, 1997).

We assumed that mapping techniques would be an efficient method in diagnosis training to develop knowledge structures for an adequate mental modelling and efficient hypotheses generation in the troubleshooting process. Mapping techniques were used in the diagnostic training to reconstruct troubleshooting knowledge in group discussions. The knowledge reconstruction was based on line troubles that were documented during the week. In an initial step, the group members wrote down all symptoms, diagnostic, and repair actions on cards that are related to the fault. Then the cards were arranged on a pin board and structured. At the end, the group considered possibilities of preventing the discussed malfunctions.

Course of the Training.   First, the goals and elements of the training were presented in detail. The training methods were explained, demonstrated, and practised, which lasted half a day. Then, the expert and novice technicians were instructed to perform troubleshooting tasks according to the cognitive apprenticeship concept. In two weekly group discussions, which each lasted for 45 minutes, the technicians reviewed and reflected on selected faults by using the mapping technique. The sessions were supervised by an external moderator. The training period lasted about six weeks.

For an initial application of the training concept, the maintenance technicians and operators of a welding transfer line, similar to the one that was used for the expertise study, were selected. A first explorative evaluation of the training programme showed that the cooperative knowledge exchange between experts and novices according to the cognitive apprenticeship approach and with support of mapping techniques had a positive impact on the individual performance (Schaper & Sonntag, 1997). The instructional methods, therefore, seemed efficiently to support the knowledge transfer from experts to novices. It can be concluded from observations of the training processes that the exchange of knowledge and experience was particularly increased through the use of mapping techniques in groups. Mapping techniques proved to be effective methods to structure and communicate complex knowledge and also to reflect on diagnostic strategies and hypotheses. Critically, application of cognitive apprenticeship components still needs to be improved. Particularly, the element of independent troubleshooting assisted by experienced maintenance technicians was only partially realized. Further research is needed to understand the causes of this deficit and to develop measures to more effectively apply elements of cognitive apprenticeship in complex technical domains.

REFERENCES

Bereiter, S.R., & Miller, S.M. (1989). A field based study of troubleshooting in computer-controlled manufacturing systems. *IEEE Transactions on Systems, Man, and Cybernetics, 19*(2), 205–219.

Chi, M., Feltovich, P.J., & Glaser, R. (1981). Categorization and representation of physics problems by experts and novices. *Cognitive Science, 5,* 121–152.

Collins, A., Brown, J.S., & Newman, E. (1989). Cognitive apprenticeship: Teaching the crafts of reading, writing and mathematics. In L.B. Resnick (Ed.), *Knowing, learning and instruction* (pp. 453–494). Hillsdale, NJ: Lawrence Erlbaum Associates Inc.

Cuny, X. (1979). Different levels of analysing process control tasks. *Ergonomics, 22,* 415–425.

Duffy, T.M., Lowyck, J., & Jonassen, D.H. (Eds). (1993). *Designing environments for constructivistic learning.* Berlin: Springer.

Elstein, A., Shulman, L.S., & Sprafka, S. (1978). *Medical problem solving: An analysis of clinical reasoning.* Cambridge, MA: Harvard University Press.

Greeno, J.G., & Simon, H.A. (1988). Problem solving and reasoning. In R.C. Atkinson, R.J. Herrnstein, J. Lindzey, & D.R. Luce (Eds), *Stevens' handbook of experimental psychology, Vol. II* (pp. 589–672). New York: Wiley.

Gruber. H., & Ziegler, A. (Eds). (1996). *Expertiseforschung.* Opladen, Germany: Westdeutscher Verlag.

Hacker, W. (1992). *Expertenkönnen. Erkennen und Vermitteln.* Göttingen, Germany: Verlag für Angewandte Psychologie.

Henneman, R., & Rouse, W.B. (1984). Measures of human problem solving performance in fault diagnosis tasks. *IEEE Transactions on Systems, Man, and Cybernetics, 14*(1), 99–12.

Hoc, J.M., & Amalberti, R. (1995). Diagnosis: Some theoretical questions raised by applied research. *Current Psychology of Cognition, 14,* 73–101.

Johnson, P.E., Hassebrock, F., Duran, A.S., & Moller, J.H. (1982). Multimethod study of clinical judgment. *Organizational Behavior of Human Performance, 30,* 201–230.

Jonassen, D.H., Beimer, K., & Yacci, M. (1993). *Structural knowledge: Techniques for representing, conveying, and acquiring structural knowledge.* Hillsdale, NJ: Lawrence Erlbaum Associates Inc.

Joseph, G.-M., & Patel, V.L. (1990). Specificity of expertise in clinical reasoning. In Cognitive Science Society (Ed.), *The Eighth Annual Conference of the Cognitive Science Society* (pp. 243–257). Hillsdale, NJ: Erlbaum.

Konradt, U. (1992). *Analyse von Strategien bei der Störungsdiagnose in der flexibel automatisierten Fertigung.* Bochum, Germany: Brockmeyer.

Krems, J., & J. Bachmaier, M. (1991). Hypothesenbildung und Strategieauswahl in Abhängigkeit vom Expertisegrad. *Zeitschrift für experimentelle und angewandte Psychologie, 38,* 394–410.

Krems, J.F. (1994). *Wissensbasierte Urteilsbildung: diagnostisches Problemlösen durch Experten und Expertensysteme.* Bern, Germany: Huber.

Lajoie, S.P., & Lesgold, A. (1992). Apprenticeship training in the workplace: Computer-coached practice environment as a new form of apprenticeship. In M.J. Farr & J. Psotka (Eds), Intelligent instruction by computer: Theory and practice (pp. 15–36). Philadelphia, PA: Taylor & Francis.

Law, L.C., & Wong, K.M.P. (1996). Expertise and Instructional Design. In H. Gruber & A. Ziegler (Eds), *Expertiseforschung. Theoretische und methodische Grundlagen* (pp. 115–147). Opladen, Germany: Westdeutscher Verlag.

Mayring, P. (1988). *Qualitative Inhaltsanalyse. Grundlagen und Techniken.* Weinheim, Germany: Deutscher Studien Verlag.

Mehle, T. (1982). Hypothesis generation in an automobile malfunction inference task. *Acta Psychologica, 52,* 87–106.

Patel, V.L., & Groen, G.I. (1991). The general and specific nature of medical expertise: A critical look. In K.A. Ericsson & J. Smith (Eds), *Toward a general theory of expertise* (pp. 93–125). Cambridge, UK: Cambridge University Press.

Patrick, J. (1993). Cognitive aspects of fault-finding, training, and transfer. *Le Traivail Humain, 56,* 187–209.

Perkins, D.N., & Solomon, G. (1989). Are cognitive skills context-bound? *Educational Researcher, 18,* 16–25.

Rasmussen, J. (1986). *Information processing and human–machine interaction: An approach to cognitive engineering.* New York: Elsevier Science Publisher.

Schaper, N. (1995). *Lernbedarfsanalyse und Trainingsgestaltung bei komplexen Diagnoseaufgaben.* Frankfurt, Germany: Peter Lang.

Schaper, N. (1997). Strukturlegetechniken zur Förderung von Wissenserwerb und -anwendung bei beruflichen Aufgaben in modernen Arbeitsstrukturen. In G. Richardt, G. Krampen, & H. Zayer (Eds), *Beiträge zur Angewandten Psychologie* (pp. 423–426). Bonn, Germany: Deutscher Psychologen Verlag.

Schaper, N., & Sonntag, K. (1995). Lembedarfsanalyse bei komplexen Aufgabenstellungen— eine inhaltsbezogene und methodenkritische Studie. *Zeitschrift für Arbeits- und Organisationspsychologie, 39,* 168–178.

Schaper, N., & Sonntag, K. (1997). Arbeitsnahe Qualifizierung für die Instandhaltung. In E. Frieling, H. Martin, & F. Tikal (Eds), *Neue Ansätze für innovative Produktionskonzepte* (pp. 227–234). Kassel, Germany: University Press.

Sonnentag, S. (1995). Excellent software professionals: Experience work activities, and perception by peers. *Behaviour and Information Technology, 14*(5), 289–299.

Sonntag, K., & Schaper, N. (Eds). (1997). *Störungsmanagement und Diagnosekompetenz. Leistungskritisches Denken und Handeln in komplexen technischen Systemen.* Zürich, Switzerland: vdf Hochschulverlag ETH Zürich.

Vessey, I. (1986). Expertise in debugging computer systems: A process analysis. *International Journal of Man–Machine Studies, 23*, 459–494.

A Commentary on "Analysis and Training of Diagnostic Expertise in Complex Technical Domains" by N. Schaper and K. Sonntag

Inge W. Brorson, Inge W. Brorson & Co., Oslo, Norway

Schaper and Sonntag in their contribution show theoretical as well as practical ambitions for this project by conducting their experiments in a real work setting. A critical question, however, should be asked with regard to a "super expert" dividing the participants into high (HP) and low performing (LP) groups: Expert evaluations in other contexts have shown variance with the results by applying purely objective criteria. It might have been "natural", instead to look at the time period between presentation of a task and its completion—a criterion which corresponds more closely with the practical demands. Of most practical interest would be, though, whether the problem is solved and in what time. The fact that both groups arrive at the right diagnosis with equal frequency might indicate that the criteria used when establishing the groups are not discriminating.

The researchers maintain that the LP group characteristically commits more deficient and more irrelevant, repeated, and/or assisted actions. If we consider the probability of deficient actions corrected for the total number instead of focusing on the pure total number, we see that the LP group has less chance to carry out irrelevant and assisted actions. In the light of this, it is incorrect to maintain a "remarkable difference" between the groups. It is the total number of deficient actions that is of primary interest here—it is of minor importance how they are categorized. Similarly, we see that the HP group has in fact a greater tendency (50%) to seek information at the control panel than the LP group (32%). This is the opposite conclusion to that drawn by the researchers. In my opinion, the main finding is that the LP group is more active and exploring than the HP group. The remaining findings are largely a function of this.

Within operant behavioural tradition, these research findings may be interpreted in a way different to the authors: For example, the apparently better performance of the HP group may to a greater degree be described as contingency governed, i.e. shaped and maintained under naturally reinforcing conditions. Remember that the HP group had more than four times more work experience than the LP group who almost without exception came "straight from school". Their behaviour may therefore be better described as purely rule governed, i.e. more "deductive" and "global". The variations in performance of the HP and the LP may therefore be more easily explained in terms of differing learning histories: The LP group has quite simply had less practical training than the HP group. Thus the HP group has basically a wider background of experience to draw upon and does not need to explore in the trial and error way the LP group does.

The researchers claim that considerable differences in performance exist between the two groups. They further assume that the LP group shows difficulties in generating an adequate mental representation of the malfunction. This could be disputed. The researchers have tended to combine both what they believe are proven training needs in the LP group and other, more general, training principles in designing a training programme. From my experience the latter would have been sufficient.

The governing consideration when putting together the training programme is that training should take place in a working situation where real problems are solved. They remind us of the importance of combining problem-solving behaviour with an explication of the operations used. Role learning with the assistance of experienced experts is very well described and the use of mapping techniques is also fascinating. There is a good deal of interesting material in this part of the article from the point of view of the practitioner.

The authors are well aware that it is impossible to draw secure conclusions about training effects on the basis of the available description. Nevertheless, many excellent and easily grasped arguments are put forward as to how a practical training programme may be set up in order to teach maintenance technicians how to tackle the problems they encounter in the workplace.

EUROPEAN JOURNAL OF WORK AND ORGANIZATIONAL PSYCHOLOGY, 1998, 7 (4), 501–515

Identifying High Performers:
Do Peer Nominations Suffer
from a Likeability Bias?

Sabine Sonnentag

University of Amsterdam, The Netherlands

This study examined whether peer nominations of high performers can be explained by the likeability of these persons. Analysis of performance and likeability ratings provided by 123 software professionals for high and average performing co-workers showed that likeability and performance ratings were positively related, but nevertheless represented to different constructs. Likeability and performance of co-workers nominated as high performers were rated higher than likeability and performance of average performing co-workers. Differences in performance ratings remained stable when taking likeability into account as a covariate. The findings suggest that peer nomination outcomes may not be reduced to likeability and that peer nominations can be regarded as one suitable method for identifying high performers within expertise research.

In recent years, interest in expertise research has increased and efforts have been made to relate this research to work settings and other areas relevant within applied psychology (Ericsson, Krampe, & Tesch-Römer, 1993; Ericsson & Lehmann, 1996; Glynn, 1996; Hesketh, 1997). Generally, expertise is defined as high and outstanding performance that is due to relatively stable individual characteristics (Ericsson & Smith, 1991). One central methodological question within expertise research refers to the measurement of high performance and the identification of high performers. It has been argued that the best indicator for expert performance is consistent superior performance on a specified set of representative tasks administered in a laboratory setting (Ericsson & Smith, 1991).

However, in many domains of expertise it is difficult to identify a standardized task that captures all aspects of expertise relevant in that domain.

Requests for reprints should be addressed to S. Sonnentag, Dept. of Psychology, University of Amsterdam, Roetersstraat 15, NL-1018 WB Amsterdam, The Netherlands; Email: ao_sonnentag@macmail.psy.uva.nl

This study was performed in the context of a research project supported by the German Research Community (DFG; So 295/1-1 and 1-2). This grant is gratefully acknowledged. I thank Harry Garst for his advice in data analysis and Doris Fay for a critical reading of the article.

Often, everyday work tasks are very complex, their accomplishment requires a long-term time frame and makes interaction with co-workers and customers necessary. Furthermore, expertise encompasses mastery of a great variety of different tasks and quick adaptation to emerging tasks (Hesketh, 1997). As a result, crucial aspects of expertise can not be captured when referring only to high performance in tasks administerable in a laboratory context. Consequently, additional approaches for measuring expertise are needed.

Peer nominations can be regarded as such an alternative expertise measure. In a number of studies, high performers were identified and nominated by their peers or other persons familiar with the person's work performance (Ericsson et al., 1993; Klemp & McClelland, 1986; Sonnentag, 1995). However, peer nominations and related approaches' have been criticized (Ericsson & Smith, 1991; Salthouse, 1991). One major objection against peer nominations and other peer assessment methods is their assumed susceptibility to popularity or likeability bias (Salthouse, 1991). On the basis of existing expertise research it can not be decided whether this objection is justified. Therefore, the present study aimed at examining the role of likeability within peer nominations.

MEASURING PERFORMANCE BY PEER ASSESSMENTS

Peer nominations are a peer assessment method. In peer assessments "members of a group judge the extent to which each of their fellow group members has exhibited specified traits, behaviors, or achievements" (Kane & Lawler, 1978, p. 555). When applying peer nominations within expertise research, co-workers within a team or a larger unit are asked to identify and name the person with the best or an exceptionally high performance.

Although not systematically examined within expertise research, peer assessments received a lot of attention within the performance appraisal literature. Within that context it is argued that peers are a good source in performance assessment because peers have extensive opportunities for observing co-workers' typical work performance and because they have access to information not available to supervisors or external raters (Borman, 1991; Reilly & Chao, 1982). Validation studies on peer assessments support this view. Lewin and Zweny (1976) summarized 15 studies on peer evaluations and reported a mean correlation of $r = 0.41$ between these evaluations and criterion measures. Kane and Lawler (1978) differentiated between various types of peer assessments. For peer nominations, Kane and Lawler reported a median correlation with criterion measures of $r = 0.43$. For peer ratings the respective correlation was $r = 0.35$. Using meta-analysis, Harris and Schaubroeck (1988) found a mean correlation of $r = 0.48$ (corrected for sampling error; $r = 0.62$ corrected for all possible artefacts) between peer and supervisory ratings. A meta-analysis reported by

Norton (1992) resulted in a mean correlation of $r = 0.48$ (uncorrected; $r = 0.69$ corrected for attenuation) between peer assessments and various criterion measures. Validity was higher for studies using objective rather than subjective criterion measures. In summary, it can be concluded that peer assessments provide fairly valid performance information.

THE ROLE OF LIKEABILITY WITHIN PEER ASSESSMENTS

Nevertheless, applying peer assessments to performance measurement is not without problems. Among other difficulties (DeNisi, Randolph, & Blencoe, 1983; Fedor, Rensvold, & Adams, 1992; McEvoy & Buller, 1987), the issue of a likeability bias has been raised (Kane & Lawler, 1978). Cardy and Dobbins (1986) pointed out that liking is an integral part of the performance rating process resulting in decreased rating accuracy. Research showed that likeability and friendship ratings are positively correlated with peer assessments of performance. In their review article, Kane and Lawler (1978) reported correlations around $r = 0.50$ between friendship and peer nominations (cf. Hollander & Webb, 1955; Waters & Waters, 1970). In more recent studies, correlations between peer nominations and friendship/likeability ratings of $r = 0.32$ and $r = 0.55$ respectively were found (Love, 1981; Petzel, Johnson, & Bresolin, 1990). For peer ratings of performance, correlations with likeability of $r = 0.22$ and $r = 0.33$ were reported (Borman, White, & Dorsey, 1995; Love, 1981). It seems that studies in which participants knew each other only for a relatively short time resulted in higher correlation coefficients (Hollander & Webb, 1955; Petzel et al., 1990) than did studies from which it can be assumed that participants already shared a longer history of working together (Borman et al., 1995; Love, 1981).

Taken together, the studies indicate that liking interferes with performance ratings and that performance of peers high on likeability is evaluated more positively than performance of less liked peers. With respect to peer nominations it can be assumed that peers who are perceived to be more likeable are more often nominated as high performers.

If one assumes a positive relationship between likeability ratings and performance ratings as well as between likeability ratings and peer nominations the question raises whether performance ratings and peer nominations reflect *more than* likeability. One could argue that within peer nomination procedures, nomination outcomes are mainly based on perceived likeability and that therefore nomination outcomes could be reduced to likeability ratings. For expertise research, this would imply that persons identified as high performers in a peer nomination procedure would not differ from non-nominated persons with respect to their performance level when controlling for likeability. The objection against peer nominations expressed within expertise research (Salthouse, 1991) is implicitly based on such a line of argument.

Until now, the assumption that peer nominations can be reduced to likeability ratings was not challenged by an empirical test. Although performance appraisal research has shown, that liking is an integral part in the appraisal process and that liking is positively related to performance ratings and peer nominations, it does not provide a clear answer to the question crucial for expertise research. It is still unknown whether peer nomination outcomes and rated performance differences remain stable when taking likeability into account.

However, two arguments speak against the assertion that peer nominations reflect nothing but likeability. First, one can assume that peer nominations are mainly based on likeability when no other information about peers' performance is available. In contrast, within real work contexts where persons work together for a longer time, peers have the opportunity to observe each others' behaviour and performance. By interacting with one another, information about peers' performance becomes available. Borman (1991) argued that it is very difficult to hide one's work performance from co-workers. Thus, within real work contexts, persons have relatively valid information available on peers' performance that they can refer to in peer nominations. This line of argument is supported by Norton's (1992) meta-analysis. Norton found that the time peers had for becoming familiar with each other showed a mean correlation of $r = 0.27$ with the validity of peer assessments. Furthermore, Borman et al. (1995) showed that in real work contexts peers base their performance ratings less on ratee likeability than on other ratee characteristics, such as technical proficiency.

Second, one can argue that nominations are based mainly on likeability when administrative consequences are resulting from the nomination outcomes. This is often the case when peer nominations are used for personnel appraisal purposes. For example, a person might anticipate that a friend will not be promoted if one does not nominate him or her as a high performer. Or a person might hesitate in nominating a peer he or she does not like because this peer might be promoted on basis of the nomination. However, when applying, peer nominations within research contexts these considerations are of minor relevance. In her meta-analysis on the validity of peer assessments, Norton (1992) found that effect sizes were higher in those studies in which peer assessments were conducted only for research purposes than they were in studies in which peer assessment data were used for administrative decision making (cf. Mabe & West, 1982 for a related argument with respect to self-evaluations). Therefore, with respect to expertise research it can be assumed that peer nominations cannot be reduced to likeability.

To summarize, existing research revealed a positive relationship between peer nomination outcomes and likeability. However, it is still unclear whether these peer nomination outcomes reflect nothing other than likeability. If this was the case, peer nominations must be abandoned within expertise research. Therefore, the present study tried to answer this question by comparing peer ratings of likeability and performance of persons identified as high performers in a peer nomination procedure with the respective ratings of persons not identified in that peer nomination procedure. When comparing peer ratings of performance it was controlled for peer ratings of likeability.

The hypotheses can be summarized as follows:

Hypothesis 1:   Likeability of persons identified as high performers in a peer nomination procedure is rated higher than likeability of persons not identified as high performers.

Hypothesis 2:   Performance of persons identified as high performers in a peer nomination procedure is rated higher than performance of persons not identified as high performers—also when controlling for likeability.

METHOD

Sample

One hundred and twenty-three software professionals participated in the study. Participants were working in 21 different software development teams from 18 organizations. The software systems developed by these teams covered a broad range of application domains, such as software systems for information and communication, process control, expert systems, graphical, and other, more specific, applications. Within these teams software professionals cooperated with one another on a daily basis. Study participants had a mean professional experience of 7.0 years (SD = 5.88). Besides typical software development activities (e.g. design, testing), 35.3% of the participants accomplished additional supervisory tasks. Mean age was 33.3 years (SD = 6.63); 21% of the sample was female. Complete data sets were available for 123 participants. Only the data of these participants were included in the analysis.

Measures

In a questionnaire, performance ratings and likeability ratings were assessed both for high and average performers. Means, standard deviations, and inter-correlations of all items can be found in Table 1. All items were in German.

Performance Rating of High Performing Co-worker. Participants were asked to think of and to nominate a real co-worker in their team they regarded as a very good software professional. Then, participants were asked to rate this co-worker's performance on a five-point Likert scale. For this performance rating, items high on face validity were developed. They were derived from an earlier study on highly performing software professionals (Sonnentag, 1995) and reflected central aspects of software development expertise (Curtis, Krasner, & Iscoe, 1988; Glass, Vessey, & Conger, 1992; Turley & Bieman, 1995): *results* (His/her work results are very good); *solutions* (He/she finds very good solutions for problems); *knowledge* (His/her technical knowledge is extensive); *problem*

TABLE 1
Means, Standard Deviations, and Intercorrelations of All Performance
and Likeability Items for High and Average Performing
Co-workers as Rating Targets

	M	SD	1	2	3	4	5	6
High performing co-worker as rating target								
1 Results	4.27	0.62						
2 Solutions	4.08	0.75	0.52					
3 Knowledge	4.20	0.71	0.42	0.53				
4 Problem analysis	4.30	0.64	0.27	0.48	0.33			
5 Working style	4.00	0.89	0.26	0.36	0.53	0.35		
6 Liking	3.99	0.82	0.30	0.29	0.24	0.14	−0.05	
7 Friendliness	3.91	0.91	0.22	0.18	0.23	0.02	−0.10	0.60
Average performing co-worker as rating target								
1 Results	3.15	0.78						
2 Solutions	2.86	0.77	0.50					
3 Knowledge	3.12	0.70	0.35	0.46				
4 Problem analysis	2.88	0.77	0.47	0.64	0.51			
5 Working style	2.81	0.92	0.55	0.32	0.20	0.30		
6 Liking	3.52	0.77	0.33	0.27	0.22	0.41	0.25	
7 Friendliness	3.47	0.99	0.38	0.28	0.19	0.35	0.17	0.76

analysis (He/she shows good problem analysis); *working style* (His/her working style is method-oriented and systematic).

Likeability Rating of High Performing Co-worker. Additionally, participants rated the likeability of this highly performing co-worker on a five-point Likert scale. The items were as follows: *liking* (I personally like him/her); *friendliness* (I have a friendly cooperative relationship with him/her).

Performance Rating of Average Performing Co-worker. Participants were asked to think of a real co-worker in their team they regarded as an average performer and to rate this person's performance. The same items and ratings formats were used as for the rating of a highly performing co-worker.

Likeability Rating of Average Performing Co-worker. Participants also rated the likeability of the co-worker regarded to be an average performer. Again, items and rating formats were the same as used for rating a highly performing co-worker.

Confirmatory Factor Analysis of Performance and Likeability Ratings. In order to examine the factor structure of the performance and likeability ratings, a confirmatory factor analysis following a LISREL approach (Jöreskog & Sörbom,

1993) was performed. Given the rather high correlations between performance and likeability ratings in previous research, it was of interest whether performance and likeability ratings represented two different constructs or whether performance and likeability ratings were indicators of one single underlying common construct. Data were analysed as follows: For both high and average performers as rating targets, the fit of three nested models was tested: null models (each item loading as the single item on one factor with that factor not being correlated to any other factor); one-factor models (all items loading on one single factor); two-factor models (items *results, solutions, knowledge, problem analysis,* and *working style* loading on a performance factor and items *liking* and *friendliness* loading on a likeability factor). χ^2-statistics and four other fit indices were computed: root mean square error of approximation (RMSEA); root mean square residual (RMSR); goodness-of-fit index (GFI); adjusted-goodness-of-fit index (AGFI); comparative-fit index (CFI). Additionally, the three nested models were directly compared by testing differences between χ^2-values (Anderson & Gerbring, 1988; Bentler, 1990). χ^2-values and fit indices for all three models and both rating targets can be found in Table 2.

Analysis showed that for both high and average performers as rating targets the one-factor models were an improvement over the null models ($\Delta\chi^2 = 154.07$; $\Delta df = 7$; $P < .001$ and $\Delta\chi^2 = 220.92$; $\Delta df = 7$; $P < .001$). Nevertheless, both one-factor models differed significantly from the data with GFIs below 0.90. Both two-factor models showed substantial improvements over the one-factor models. For the high and average performing co-worker as rating targets the difference between χ^2-scores of the one-factor and the two-factor model were $\Delta\chi^2 = 48.32$ ($\Delta df = 1$; $P < .001$) and $\Delta\chi^2 = 80.32$ ($\Delta df = 1$; $P < .001$) respectively. The fit

TABLE 2

Fit Statistics for Null, One-factor, and Two-factor Models of Performance and Likeability for High and Average Performing Co-workers as Rating Targets

Model	χ^2	df	P	RMSEA	RMSR	GFI	AGFI	CFI
High performing co-worker as rating target (N=123)								
Null	222.73	21	0.000	0.280	0.280	0.61	0.48	0.00
One factor	68.66	14	0.000	0.180	0.120	0.86	0.73	0.73
Two factor	20.34	13	0.087	0.068	0.070	0.95	0.90	0.96
Average performing co-worker as rating target (N=123)								
Null	337.85	21	0.000	0.350	0.350	0.50	0.34	0.00
One factor	116.93	14	0.000	0.250	0.110	0.81	0.62	0.68
Two factor	36.61	13	0.00048	0.120	0.062	0.93	0.84	0.93

RMSEA = root mean square error of approximation; RMSR = root mean square residiual; GFI = goodness-of-fit index; AGFI = adjusted-goodness-of-fit index; CFI = comparative-fit index.

indices for the high performing co-worker were satisfying (Schumacker & Lomax, 1996) and were substantially better than those attained with the one-factor model. For the average performing co-worker as rating target the results were less satisfying, but still showed a reasonable fit. Maximum likelihood estimates for the factor loadings of the two-factor models ranged from 0.40 to 0.99 and were all significant at $P < .01$.

This overall superiority of the two-factor models over the one-factor models clearly shows that performance and likeability ratings were indicators of different constructs. However, there were substantial correlations between the two latent variables for both rating targets. The correlations between the performance and likeability factor were 0.35 ($SE = 0.11$; $t = 3.20$) for the high performing co-worker and 0.50 ($SE = 0.09$; $t = 5.85$) for the average performing co-worker, indicating that co-workers rated high on likeability were also rated high on performance.

For further analyses, the items *results, solutions, knowledge, problem analysis,* and *working style* were combined into a measure of performance (Cronbach's alpha = 0.74 for the high performing co-worker as rating target and 0.78 for the average performing co-worker as rating target). The likeability measure was based on the items *liking* and *friendliness* ($r = .60$ for the performing co-worker as rating target and $r = .76$ for the average performing co-worker as rating target).

Interrater Agreement of Peer Ratings and Validity of Peer Nomination. Interrater agreement was computed for performance and likeability ratings given for high performers. The procedure suggested by James, Demaree, and Wolf (1984) was used. Mean interrater reliability was 0.90 for performance ratings and 0.89 for likeability ratings. One could argue that ratings provided for someone perceived as a high performer might suffer from a leniency bias. After controlling for a moderate leniency bias, mean interrater reliability was 0.70 for performance ratings and 0.67 for likeability ratings. For average performers as rating target, no interrater agreement could be computed because the data did not provide enough information necessary for this procedure.

In a separate study, the relationship between peer nomination outcomes and performance in a software design task was tested. Analysis showed that highly performing software designers identified by a peer nomination method similar to the procedure described here showed a substantially better design task performance than software designers assumed to be average performers (Sonnentag, in press). The size of the effect ($d = 0.80$) was in line with other validity coefficients of peer assessments (Harris & Schaubroeck, 1988; Kane & Lawler, 1978; Lewin & Zwany, 1976; Norton, 1992) and indicates that this peer nomination method is related to hard performance criteria.

RESULTS

Hypotheses were tested by comparing performance and likeability ratings provided for high and average performers with multivariate analysis of variance (MANOVA) and subsequent univariate analysis of variance (ANOVA) and covariance (ANCOVA). Within all analyses a repeated measurement approach was followed with rating target as repeated measurement factor. Means and standard deviation of performance and likeability measures are shown in Table 3.

Multivariate analysis of variance showed that highly performing co-workers were assessed more positively by their colleagues than were co-workers regarded to be average performers, $F(1, 122) = 227.78$; $P < .001$. Additionally, the difference between performance and likeability ratings, $F(1, 122) = 7.19$; $P < .01$, and the interaction effect, $F(1, 122) = 66.34$; $P = .001$, were significant. This interaction effect indicated that the difference between the ratings provided for high vs. average performing co-workers was bigger for performance ratings ($M = 1.21$; $SD = 0.60$) than it was for likeability ratings ($M = 0.45$; $SD = 0.96$; $t(122) = 8.14$; $P < .001$).

Subsequent univariate analysis of variance showed that co-workers regarded as high performers were rated more positively with respect to likeability, $F(1, 122) = 27.35$; $P < .001$; $\eta^2 = 0.18$. Thus, Hypothesis 1, assuming higher likeability ratings for persons identified as high performers than for persons identified as average performers, was supported by the data.

Performance of co-workers regarded to be high performers was rated higher than performance of co-workers seen as average performers, $F(1, 122) = 500.15$; $P < .001$; $\eta^2 = 0.80$. Because it could not be excluded that these more positive performance ratings provided for high performers were due to more favourable likeability ratings, analysis of covariance was performed with likeability as a covariate. A significant effect of the covariate likeability on performance ratings was found, $F(1, 121) = 4.29$; $P < .05$. Nevertheless, the differences in per-

TABLE 3

Performance and Likeability Ratings for High and Average Performing
Co-workers as Rating Targets—Results from Analyses
of Variance and Covariance

	High Performing Co-worker		Average Performing Co-worker		ANOVA	ANCOVA[a]
	M	SD	M	SD	F(1,122)	F(1,121)
Performance	4.17	0.50	2.96	0.58	500.15**	384.05**
Likeability	3.95	0.78	3.50	0.89	27.35**	–

$*P < .05$; $**P < .01$; [a]analyses of covariance with likeability rating as covariate.

formance ratings between co-workers regarded as high vs. average performers remained stable when taking likeability into account as covariate, $F(1, 121) = 384.05$; $P < .001$; $\eta^2 = 0.76$. This indicates that the more positive performance ratings given for high performers can not be explained by more positive likeability ratings. Thus, Hypothesis 2, assuming higher performance ratings for persons regarded as high performers than for persons identified as average performers—irrespective of likeability—was supported by the data.

DISCUSSION

The study showed that performance and likeability of persons nominated as high performers was rated higher than performance and likeability of persons regarded to be average performers. Differences in performance ratings remained stable when controlling for likeability. Thus, the study supported both hypotheses.

Results confirm findings of earlier studies showing moderate positive relationships between likeability or friendship ratings on the one hand and peer assessments of performance on the other hand (Borman et al., 1995; Kane & Lawler, 1978; Love, 1981). The present study adds to existing research by showing that nominations of high performers correspond to high performance ratings provided for these nominated persons and that these performance ratings can not be explained by the fact that these co-workers are at the same time regarded as more likeable. Taken together, present findings suggest that— although empirically related—likeability is not the key variable to which peer nomination outcomes can be attributed.

A similar conclusion can be derived from a recent validation study by Schmitt, Pulakos, Nason, and Whitney (1996). The authors reported positive relationships between likeability and predictors of performance, but found no effect of such a bias on the relationship between predictors and criterion. When applying this finding to peer assessments one can conclude that—despite the existence of a likeability bias—validity of peer assessment does not suffer much from such a bias.

Additionally, measurement models tested in the study showed that ratings of likeability and performance represented two different constructs—both for high and average performers. This indicates that peers differentiate between likeability and performance of a co-worker.

In the present study *one* rater provided peer nominations, performance, and likeability ratings. One might argue that it was necessary that peer nominations, performance, and likeability ratings were given by different raters. Such a procedure was often followed in the context of performance rating research (e.g. VanScotter & Motowidlo, 1996) and is an appropriate strategy when examining the predictive validity of various performance aspects. However, predictive validity was not the purpose of the present study. In the present study it was tested whether peer nominations are exclusively based on likeability or whether nominated and not nominated peers differ with respect to perceived performance when controlling for likeability. As a matter of fact, when controlling for likeability all common variance between likeability and performance attributable to raters' characteristics or the method used was already controlled for as well. In a case in which performance and likeability ratings were provided by different raters, the probability that differences between peers nominated and not nominated would remain stable when controlling for likeability would be greater. Thus, with the procedure followed in the present study a more stringent test for the hypothesis was chosen.

One can assume that most teams consisted of only a few high performers, but a great number of average performers. The present study does not provide information about the processes involved in choosing a specific average performing co-worker as rating target. It might be that participants chose a friend or another familiar person as the average performing co-worker. As a consequence, likeability ratings for this person would be relatively high. However, the study showed that—compared to high performers—even chosen average performers were rated relatively low on likeability. This suggests that not-chosen average performers were perceived even as less likeable than those for whom performance and likeability ratings were provided. Alternatively, one might argue that participants did not comply with the instruction and chose *weak* instead of *average* performers for the ratings. This interpretation can not be ruled out completely. However, inspection of performance ratings shows that mean ratings varied closely around a score of three on the five-point-scales suggesting that participants did rate an average performing co-worker's performance.

Likeability Reconsidered

Within cross-sectional designs such as in the present study, there are several interpretations for the higher likeability ratings provided for co-workers regarded as high performers. First, it is possible that peers who are perceived to be friendly and likeable are more often seen as high performers and their performance is rated more positively *because of* this perceived friendliness and likeability. This implies that likeability works as a "hot cognition" (Zajonc, 1980) in the assessment process resulting in biased nominations and performance ratings. Although there is empirical evidence for such an inference between likeability and performance assessment (Cardy & Dobbins, 1886), the present study clearly showed that outcomes of performance ratings can not be reduced to likeability.

Second, one can argue that likeability is effected by performance, i.e. someone showing high performance is *perceived* to be more likeable. This interpretation put forward by Robbins and DeNisi (1994) makes sense in teamwork settings such as encountered in the present study: When a software professional shows high performance, i.e. finishes the work quickly and at a high quality level, cooperation with this person is more easy than with another colleague whose work products are of lower quality and therefore subsequently might cause difficulties for the whole team. Smooth cooperation with a high performer might increase likeability while facing frequent problems with a co-worker might reduce likeability.

Third, the finding that co-workers nominated as high performers were described to be more likeable might not only reflect biased performance assessments or biased likeability ratings but also a "true" relationship with likeability being an aspect of high performance (Schmitt, 1994). One can imagine situations involving a high degree of social interaction where likeability facilitates high performance. Again, in work settings requiring cooperation, likeability can help in attaining a high level of individual performance. For example, a friendly person who gets along well with co-workers might receive necessary information more easily and will be less involved in conflicts. This will result in this person's efficient working processes and high performance.

Consequences for Expertise Research

With respect to expertise research, two conclusions become obvious. First, persons identified as high performers were at the same time described as being more likeable than persons not identified. Although the exact causal processes are still unclear, this finding points in the same direction as did research on the relationship between personality and performance in which a weak positive correlation between agreeableness and performance was found (Tett, Jackson, & Rothstein, 1991). At the same time, this finding questions the rather negative description of experts put forward by Shanteau (1988) who characterized expert decision makers as "egotistical, self-important, and overconfident" (p. 211). It seems that particularly in team-work settings and related work contexts likeability and high performance are intertwined to a certain degree.

Second, the present study showed that performance of persons identified as high performers was rated higher also when controlling for likeability. This implies that the assumption that peer nominations reflect only likeability or popularity can not be sustained. Nevertheless, the question of validity of peer assessments remains a crucial one. In the performance appraisal literature uncorrected correlation coefficients between peer assessments and criterion measures ranging from $r = 0.35$ to $r = 0.48$ were reported (Harris & Schaubroeck, 1988; Kane & Lawler, 1978; Lewin & Zwany, 1976; Norton, 1992). Similarly, a recent study on expertise in software design showed that peer nominations and objective performance in a specific task were clearly related to but did not overlap completely (Sonnentag, in press). However, this does not speak against the validity of peer assessments because one might not expect a perfect relationship between performance measures on very different specificity levels (cf. Epstein & O'Brien, 1985). Rather, the moderate relationship between peer nominations and specific task performance suggests that peer nominations and task performance measures cover different aspects of high performance. Although task performance is often regarded to be the preferable performance measure (Ericsson & Smith, 1991), peer nominations offer additional advantages such as the possibility to assess performance with respect to a longer time frame and a broader range of tasks and activities. Therefore, as a consequence for expertise research, it can be concluded that peer nominations should not replace specific task performance measures—or vice versa. In order to arrive at internally and externally valid measures of high performance it is recommended to combine task performance measures with peer assessments.

Implications for Human Resource Management

In the present study, peer nomations were assessed in a research context. Therefore, caution is required when drawing conclusions for applied purposes such as personnel selection. From the present study it can not be excluded that likeability does have an effect on peer nomination outcomes when administrative decisions are based on these nominations. Nevertheless, some authors are rather optimistic about the use of peer assessments for personnel selection purposes (Cardy & Dobbins, 1994; Reilly & Chao, 1982). In order to cope with likeability bias that might be partially based on similarity (cf. Wayne & Liden, 1995), Dobson (1989) suggests to conduct peer appraisals in groups which are homogenous with respect to race, sex, and socio-economic background.

Task requirements in today's work organizations are permanently changing. In order to design effective training programmes for these changing situations, organizations need information about knowledge and skills necessary for successful task accomplishment. Peer nominations are an economic approach to identify employees working on a high performance level. After having identified high performers, these employees' approaches to task accomplishment can be studied and further used for developing training programmes. The present study provided useful information for such an endeavour by showing that peer nomination outcomes can not be reduced to likeability.

REFERENCES

Anderson, J.C., & Gerbring, D.W. (1988). Structural equation modeling in practice: A review and recommended two-step approach. *Psychological Bulletin, 103*, 411–423.

Bentler, P.M. (1990). Comparative fit indices in structural models. *Psychological Bulletin, 107*, 238–246.

Borman, W.C. (1991). Job behavior, performance, and effectiveness. In M.D. Dunnette & L.M. Hough (Eds), *Handbook of industrial and organizational psychology* (Vol. 2, pp. 271–326). Palo Alto, CA: Consulting Psychologists Press.

Borman, W.C., White, L.A., & Dorsey, D.W. (1995). Effects of ratee task performance and interpersonal factors on supervisor and peer performance ratings. *Journal of Applied Psychology, 80*, 168–177.

Cardy, R.L., & Dobbins, G.H. (1986). Affect and appraisal accuracy: Liking as an integral dimension in evaluating performance. *Journal of Applied Psychology, 71*, 672–678.

Cardy, R.L., & Dobbins, G.H. (1994). *Performance appraisal: Alternative perspectives.* Cincinnati, OH: South-Western Publishing.

Curtis, B., Krasner, H., & Iscoe, N. (1988). A field study of the software design process for large systems. *Communications of the ACM, 31*, 1268–1287.

DeNisi, A.S., Randolph, W.A., & Blencoe, A.G. (1983). Potential problems with peer ratings. *Academy of Management Journal, 26*, 457–464.

Dobson, P. (1989). Self and peer assessment. In P. Herriot (Ed.), *Assessment and selection in organizations* (pp. 421–432). Chichester, UK: Wiley.

Epstein, S., & O'Brien, E.J. (1985). The person–situation debate in historical and current perspective. *Psychological Bulletin, 98*, 513–537.

Ericsson, K.A., Krampe, R.T., & Tesch-Römer, C. (1993). The role of deliberate practice in the acquisition of expert performance. *Psychological* Review, *100*, 363–406.

Ericsson, K.A., & Lehmann, A.C. (1996). Expert and exceptional performance: Evidence of maximal adaptation to task constraints. *Annual Review of Psychology, 47*, 273–305.

Ericsson, K.A., & Smith, J. (1991). Prospects and limits of the empirical study of expertise: An introduction. In K.A. Ericsson & J. Smith (Ed), *Toward a general theory of expertise: Prospects and limits* (pp. 1–38). Cambridge, UK: Cambridge University Press.

Fedor, D.B., Rensvold, R.B., & Adams, S.M. (1992). An investigation of factors expected to affect feedback seeking: A longitudinal field study. *Personnel Psychology, 45*, 779–805.

Glass, R.L., Vessey, I., & Conger, S.A. (1992). Software tasks: Intellectual or clerical? *Information and Management, 23*, 183–191.

Glynn, M.A. (1996). Innovative genius: A framework for relating individual and organizational intelligences to innovation. *Academy of Management Review, 21*, 1081–1111.

Harris, M.M., & Schaubroeck, J. (1988). A meta-analysis of self-supervisor, self-peer, and peer-supervisor ratings. *Personnel Psychology, 41*, 43–62.

Hesketh, B. (1997). Dilemmas in training for transfer and retention. *Applied Psychology: An International Review, 46*, 317–386.

Hollander, E.P., & Webb, W.B. (1955). Leadership, followership, and friendship: An analysis of peer nominations. *Journal of Abnormal and Social Psychology, 50*, 163–167.

James, L.R., Demaree, R.G., & Wolf, G. (1984). Estimating within-group interrater reliability with and without response bias. *Journal of Applied Psychology, 69*, 85–98.

Jöreskog, K.G., & Sörbom, D. (1993). *LISREL 8: Structural equation modeling with the SIMPLIS command language.* Hillsdale, NJ: Lawrence Erlbaum Associates Inc.

Kane, J.S., & Lawler, E.E. (1978). Methods of peer assessment. *Psychological Bulletin, 85*, 555–586.

Klemp, G.O., & McClelland, D.C. (1986). What characterizes intelligent functioning among senior managers? In R.J. Sternberg & R.K. Wagner (Eds), *Practical intelligence: Nature and origin of competence in the everyday world* (pp. 31–50). Cambridge, UK: Cambridge University Press.

Lewin, A.Y., & Zwany, A. (1976). Peer nominations: A model, literature critique and a paradigm for research. *Personnel Psychology, 29*, 423–447.

Love, K.G. (1981). Comparison of peer assessment methods: Reliability, validity, friendship bias, and user reaction. *Journal of Applied Psychology, 66*, 451–457.

Mabe, P.M., & West, S.G. (1982). Validity of self-evaluations of ability. *Journal of Applied Psychology, 67*, 180–196.

McEvoy, G.M., & Buller, P.F. (1987). User acceptance of peer appraisals in an industrial setting. *Personnel Psychology, 40*, 783–797.

Norton, S.M. (1992). Peer assessments of performance and ability: An exploratory meta-analysis of statistical artifacts and contextual moderators. *Journal of Business and Psychology, 6*, 387–399.

Petzel, T.P., Johnson, J.E., & Bresolin, L. (1990). Peer nominations for leadership and likeability in problem-solving groups as a function of gender and task. *Journal of Social Psychology, 130*, 641–648.

Reilly, R.R., & Chao, G.T. (1982). Validity and fairness of some alternative employee selection procedures. *Personnel Psychology, 35*, 1–61.

Robbins, T.L., & DeNisi, A.S. (1994). A closer look at interpersonal affect as a distinct influence on cognitive processing in performance evaluations. *Journal of Applied Psychology, 79*, 341–353.

Salthouse, T.A. (1991). Expertise as the circumvention of human processing limitations. In K.A. Ericsson & J. Smith (Eds), *Prospects and limits of the empirical study of expertise: An introduction* (pp. 286–300). Cambridge, UK: Cambridge University Press.

Schmitt, N. (1994). Method bias: The importance of theory and measurement. *Journal of Organizational Behavior, 15*, 393–398.

Schmitt, N., Pulakos, E.D., Nason, E., & Whitney, D.J. (1996). Likeability and similarity as potential sources of predictor-related criterion bias in validation research. *Organizational Behavior and Human Decision Processes, 68*, 272–286.

Schumacker, R.E., & Lomax, R.G. (1996). *A beginner's guide to structural equation modeling.* Mahwah, NJ: Lawrence Erlbaum Associates Inc.

Shanteau, J. (1988). Psychological characteristics and strategies of expert decision makers. *Acta Psychologica, 68*, 203–215.

Sonnentag, S. (1995). Excellent software professionals: Experience, work activities, and perceptions by peers. *Behaviour and Information Technology, 14*, 289–299.

Sonnentag, S. (in press). Expertise in professional software design: A process study. *Journal of Applied Psychology.*

Tett, R.P., Jackson, D.N., & Rothstein, M. (1991). Personality measures as predictors of job performance: A meta-analytic review. *Personnel Psychology, 44*, 703–742.

Turley, R.T., & Bieman, J.M. (1995). Competencies of exceptional and nonexeptional software engineers. *Journal of Systems and Software, 28*, 19–38.

VanScotter, J.R., & Motowidlo, S.J. (1996). Interpersonal facilitation and job dedication as seperate facets of contextual performance. *Journal of Applied Psychology, 81*, 525–531.

Waters, L.K., & Waters, C.W. (1970). Peer nominations as predictors of short-term sales performance. *Journal of Applied Psychology, 54*, 42–44.

Wayne, S.J., & Liden, R.C. (1995). Effects of impression management on performance ratings: A longitudinal study. *Academy of Management Journal, 38*, 232–260.

Zajonc, R.B. (1980). Feelings and thinking: Preferences need no inferences. *American Psychologist, 35*, 151–175.

A Commentary on "Identifying High Performers: Do Peer Nominations Suffer from a Likeability Bias?" by S. Sonnentag

Victor Pérez Velasco, PGP Consultores, Madrid, Spain

This article gives—viewed from the practitioner's perspective—some fruitful hints on a very interesting topic. Globally it links two positive items at the workplace: likeability and peer assessment. Likeability is positive because it helps to create a good working climate and a motivated attitude towards work. Peer assessments are the highlight of every workplace survey and therefore are always welcome as one way to find out talents and high performers, though not the main path for it. Likeability plus peer assessments could be an additional tool for managers and organizations assessing their staff. But—as the reported study tell us—this combination also presents limitations: Sometimes likeability does not get to the results we would desire.

Thus, to extract the positive effects for practical application the main target must be to neutralize the undesirable effects of both likeability and peer nominations by means of an adequate strategy. In order to find this, one might design studies combining the following actions: evaluation, training, implementation, follow-up. In practical terms this means to isolate a sample and define actions and measurements including the former four techniques: (1) evaluate friendship and peer relationships; (2) train the employees involved to look at topics in favour of increased objectivity; (3) perform; (4) use peer assessments as a tool and means to control the results and feedback.

The main target in order to produce practical value should be to get a balance between knowledge and change. The procedure to be found should obtain the best from likeability plus the best from peer assessments. It should link both concepts in a tool which avoids the negative effects by means of evaluating, training, implementing positive results, and following up the experience. This contribution shows the added value possible by transferring the results from scientific studies to the applied field—thus, chaining theory and practice.

EUROPEAN JOURNAL OF WORK AND ORGANIZATIONAL PSYCHOLOGY, 1998, 7 (4), 517–531

Competencies for Work Domains in Business Computer Science

Peter T. van den Berg

Tilburg University, The Netherlands

In order to relate expertise in business computer science to multiple criteria, the importance of competencies, as elements of expertise, for the performance of tasks and roles were investigated. Seventy-five information technology professionals (nine women and sixty-six men) from twenty-one organizations rated the importance of thirty-four competencies for the performance of eighty-six tasks and seven roles. In accordance with previous studies, knowledge of information technology, working methodically, and analytic ability were rated as important competencies for most types of tasks, and social skills were especially important for tasks related to interaction with the environment and leadership roles. By means of cluster analysis, four work domains were discerned: technique-oriented, organization-oriented, leadership-oriented, and user-support-oriented domains. It is argued that relating competencies to work domains has theoretical and practical relevance.

More and more organizations realize that their most important competitive advantage is the knowledge, skills, and abilities of their employees. Because of the globalization of the world economy, everything can be produced nearly everywhere. The only things that are difficult to imitate or to transfer are the characteristics of the people who are important for organization's success. In this context, expertise is potentially an important concept for organizations.

As stated in the Introduction to this issue, expertise is defined in terms of "what distinguishes outstanding individuals in a domain from less outstanding individuals in that domain, as well as from people in general" (Ericsson & Smith, 1991, p. 2). This should be developed further to enhance scientific understanding and to make it more applicable to human resource management of modern

Requests for reprints should be addressed to P.T. van den Berg, Work and Organization Research Centre, Tilburg University, P.O. Box 90153, 5000 LE Tilburg, The Netherlands; Email: p.t.vandenberg@kub.nl

The study was supported by a grant from the Dutch Computer Society.

The author wishes to thank S. Sonnentag and two anonymous reviewers for their comments on an earlier version of the article and the members of the research team: P.J.T. van der Kamp, J.I. Keizer, J.C. Op de Coul, M.A.M. Felt, H.H. Laferte, A. van Nouhuijs, G.P.A. Peeters, P. Waleboer, R.J.A. Kunzler, and E.J.E. Meijers for their assistance.

organizations. Therefore, the work domain to which expertise is related should be defined more clearly. Several methods are used for identifying experts, as such length of experience, overall appraisal of performance, and peer nominations, but in all studies known to the author the expertise concept has been used to indicate a general level of job performance. This means that expertise has been linked to a composite criterion. As Schmidt and Kaplan (1971) noted, a composite criterion may represent an economic dimension, but for the scientific understanding of behaviour multiple criteria should be used.

Developments in modern organizations make multiple criteria also more valuable for applied human resource management. Nowadays, employees often change tasks within the same job because they work on temporary projects. This is especially true in computer science (Bridges, 1994). This means that human resource management should focus on continuously matching the characteristics of the employees with the work activities to be done. This process may start in the personnel selection phase. In the case of a narrow labour market, applicants do not need to have all the job requirements. However, they have to have some basic traits and be able to improve other characteristics by training. When contracted, they have to find their way in the organization by comparing the characteristics they have with the characteristics that will be required in the future and then try to acquire what they are lacking. In this process, they should be helped to seek out tasks they like to perform and that will become more and more important for the organization in the future. This can make clear which competencies they will need to improve in order to perform well in a new composition of tasks, so that they increase their employability. To help employees in making career choices, it makes sense to describe the work domains in which they can be an expert.

In order to distinguish several expertise domains, the concept of competency will be used. Competency is a key concept in modern personnel management. Spencer and Spencer (1993, p. 9) defined competency as "an underlying characteristic of an individual that is causally related to criterion-referenced effective and/or superior performance in a job or situation". Several methods are available for establishing the characteristics of outstanding workers, e.g. critical incident interview, repertory grid method, and analysis of work activities. A competency consists of a definition and a description of the specific behaviours in which the competency is demonstrated. Competencies can be considered the basic elements of expertise. As a special characteristic of competencies, they can be used for assessing the individual as well as his or her performance on the job. Therefore, they are suited for distinguishing expertise or competency domains and for describing the characteristics of experts.

A growing occupational sector in which the trends described earlier are predominant is computer science. A lot of studies have been performed on the characteristics of experts in this field. Experienced programmers showed more abstract representation of problems (Weiser & Shertz, 1983) and more metacognitive knowledge of tasks and strategies (Eteläpelto, 1993) than inexperienced subjects. High performers on experimental tasks spent more time evaluating problems and solutions (Vessey, 1986). Exceptional designers in software projects were able to integrate their thorough knowledge of the application domain with their computer knowledge and showed excellent communication skills and high motivation (Curtis, Krasner, & Iscoe, 1988). Sonnentag (1995) found that excellent software professionals have high technical knowledge and a high level of social skills, and use a method-oriented working style. They also spend more time on review meetings and consultations.

Some studies on competencies relate to information technology professionals. For example, Spencer and Spencer (1993) found that the following competencies, in descending order of importance, contribute to superior performance of technicians and professionals: achievement orientation, impact and influence, conceptual thinking, analytical thinking, initiative, self-confidence, interpersonal understanding, concern for order, information-seeking, teamwork and co-operation, expertise, and customer service orientation. Interestingly, communicative and motivational factors turned out to be more important than cognitive factors.

The studies cited make only a general distinction between high-flyers and other people without referring to the specific contents of their work. However, people who are experts in some domain of work may be non-experts in another domain. As noted before, it would be better to define the work domains to which expertise might be related. This is done in the present study.

Besides the content of the job, contextual variables may contribute to the validity of competencies. Many studies show that in some types of situations, so-called "weak" situations, behavioural characteristics are more important than in other types of situations, so-called "strong" situations. This distinction is related to the concept of autonomy. For example, Barrick and Mount (1991) found that, in management jobs with a high level of autonomy, high scores on con-scientiousness and extraversion and low scores on agreeableness are more strongly related to high performance than in low-autonomy jobs. Therefore, work autonomy was considered an important contextual variable.

THE PRESENT STUDY

The aim of the present study is to investigate the importance of competencies for the performance of work activities in business computer science and to discern work domains consisting of tasks and roles requiring similar competencies, i.e. expertise domains. For this purpose, the work activities in this sector were divided into a number of tasks and roles. Next, information technology professionals rated the importance of some frequently used competencies for their own tasks and roles. This method is similar to Guion's (1965) synthetic validity method. To investigate the validity of a test battery in small sample sizes, Guion divided the activities and responsibilities in an organization into some elements and related the test scores to the performance of the employees on the elements composing their job. In the present study, the actual levels of competencies and performances were not measured, but the relationships were rated subjectively. This was done for the following reasons. Many measures of competencies and performance lack the necessary reliability. The actual performance of knowledge workers is mostly invisible for their managers. In their meta-analysis, Mabe and West (1982) found that self-ratings show high differentiation between dimensions, suggesting that job incumbents have the best knowledge of their job contents. Besides, the purpose of the study was not to validate the competencies, but to explore the expertise domains in business computer science.

Although the present study is mainly descriptive, some general hypotheses were formulated on the basis of the studies cited. The following competencies were assumed to be important for the performance of many tasks and roles: knowledge of information technology, cognitive ability, working methodically, and motivation. Social skills were hypothesized to be important for the execution of tasks requiring interaction with the environment and for the performance of leadership roles. This expectation follows from the meta-analysis by Barrick and Mount (1991) showing that extraversion predicts performance in occupations requiring interaction with other people. This is in accordance with the fact that, in the study by Sonnentag (1995) on the social skills of experts, 51.3% of them were team or subteam leaders.

METHOD

Sample and Procedure

A pilot study was performed to test whether the administration of the instrument of the main study caused any trouble and whether any improvements were needed. The sample consisted of 11 information technology professionals from a Belgian firm. They filled in the questionnaire and made suggestions for improvement.

The sample in the main study consisted of 75 professionals in business computer science from 21 organizations. The organizations were approached by phone and by letter for participation in the study. When an organization agreed to cooperate, a questionnaire was distributed to the employees working in business computer science. The completed questionnaires were sent to the investigator in a postage-paid envelope. Anonymity of the participants was guaranteed. They held the following jobs: 12 informatics consultants, 9 applications programmers, 10 systems programmers, 9 network/data managers, 9 system designers, 2 information analysts, 14 information managers/coordinators, and 5 project leaders. Four jobs could not be classified. The mean number of years in the current job was 4.9 ($SD = 5.1$). Their age ranged from 24 to 59 with a mean age of 36 ($SD = 8.9$). There were 9 women and 66 men.

Measures

Tasks. A typology of tasks in business computer science was used that was developed by the Dutch Computer Society (1993) and is presented in the Appendix. It consists of descriptions of 86 tasks comprising the whole field of business computer science. A task was defined as a group of activities that yield an intended result and cannot reasonably be split up. On the basis of the main concerns of the tasks, they were divided into nine groups as shown in the Appendix. These groups of tasks represent aspects of information management. The aspects of data, functions, facilities, organization, and coordination were derived from Zachman's (1987) architecture model, and the aspect of co-ordination consists of tasks coordinating these four aspects. The aspects of quality control, project control, business management, and interaction with the environment were added by the Dutch Computer Society (1993) to describe tasks regulating the relationships between the organization of information manage-ment and other business functions. The subjects were asked to indicate the tasks they performed.

Roles. In business computer science, many tasks can be done within the scope of different roles, and this scope may yield additional required com-petencies. For example, the task "Composition of project report" may be done in the role of a person who has to propose new solutions (creative role) or in the role of an assistant who has to describe the ideas of others. In the present study, the following roles were used: the decision-making role, the consultative role, the creative role, the reconnaissance role, the stimulating-leadership role, the directive-leadership role, and the assisting role. Descriptions of these roles were presented, and the subjects were asked to indicate the roles they performed in their job.

Importance of Competencies. The job requirements mentioned in 100 advertisements for information technology professionals were categorized in 30 groups. Four additional requirements were formulated by experienced IT pro-fessionals who participated in the research team. Behavioural descriptions of the 34 competencies were derived from competency models described in the re-search literature. On the basis of consensus in the research team, a distinction was made between competencies that are assumed to be trainable and competencies that are assumed difficult to change. Trainable competencies are not necessarily required in personnel selection, but may be acquired to some degree later on. Stable competencies, on the other hand, should be present beforehand. Cognitive competencies were also distinguished from behavioural competencies, as they are usually measured with other methods. This resulted in the following groups of competencies: (1) knowledge (trainable, cognitive): knowledge of IT, knowl-edge of other disciplines, knowledge of the environment, and commercial insight; (2) behavioural style (trainable, behavioural): planning and organizing, group leadership, individual leadership, conflict handling, resoluteness, convincingness, didactic skills, initiative, independence, communicative skills, oral fluency, writing skills, teamwork, negotiating skills, customer orientedness, working methodically, accuracy, and listening; (3) cognitive capacity (stable, cognitive): abstraction ability, problem analysis, judgement, creativity, and analytic ability; and (4) personality (stable, behavioural): perseverance, flexibility, emotional stability, immunity to stress, sensitivity, need for achievement, and integrity.

The competencies were presented in a random order. Descriptions of these competencies were also provided. The subjects were asked to rate the importance of the competencies for high performance on the tasks and roles they accomplished on a scale ranging from 0 (not important) to 3 (very important).

Autonomy. The level of autonomy was measured with the following three items: (1) you have to work following the prescriptions of supervisors, (2) you can independently take decisions about your own work activities, and (3) there is ample scope for the contribution of your own ideas. These items were rated on vertical bars with, on the left-hand side, the numbers one to nine and, on the right-hand side eight job names that indicated the levels on the bars. The levels of the eight jobs were derived from the ratings of seven experts (see Van den Berg & Feij, 1993). In order to obtain a reliable score on autonomy, the item scores were added up. The Cronbach's alpha of the composite autonomy scale in the present study was 0.67.

RESULTS

Because the number of tasks and roles of each subject was limited, not all the subjects rated all the tasks and roles. The mean number of subjects per task was 16.5 ($SD = 6.8$), and the mean number of subjects per role was 35.9 ($SD = 14.2$). Although some tasks were rated by a small number of subjects, the standard error of the mean of nearly all the tasks fell within the limits of a half point on the four-point scales and the 95% confidence intervals were smaller than 1.

The Cronbach's alpha was used as an indication of agreement among raters. The data matrix with the importance scores of the competencies for each task and role was transposed, resulting in 93 matrices with subjects as variables and competencies as cases. The mean of the 93 Cronbach's alphas was 0.85. This result shows that the profiles of the scores among the raters are very similar, although the absolute scores may differ.

For each of the 86 tasks, the mean importance of the competencies was calculated. These results are too extensive to be presented here. First, in order to reduce the number of competencies without losing relevant information, a cluster analysis was performed on the mean importance scores. Four pairs of competencies were clustered because they were conceptually similar and had nearly the same ratings: group leadership and individual leadership; methodical work and accuracy; abstraction ability and problem analysis; and emotional stability and immunity to stress. Second, within the nine groups of task (see Appendix), the mean importance scores were averaged. In order to investigate the agreement of the task ratings within groups, the Cronbach's alphas were calculated using tasks as variables and competencies as cases. The mean alpha was 0.88 ($SD = 0.09$) and the lowest was 0.72 for the Business management group. These results show that aggregation of the scores within the groups was allowed. Because the tasks were not rated by the same subjects, the importance scores within these groups were based on variable groups of subjects. The results are presented in Table 1.

In accordance with the hypotheses, knowledge of information technology and working methodically/accuracy were considered to be important competencies for the performance of nearly all the groups of tasks. The cognitive capacities of analytic ability and, to a lesser degree, abstraction ability/problem analysis were also rated as important in most groups. Judgement and creativity reached the importance score of 2 or higher in fewer groups, but it may be argued that these competencies are less central aspects of general cognitive capacity. Also in accordance with the expectations was the finding that, in the group of interaction with the environment, most competencies involving social skills were rated as important or very important. However, the results with respect to the importance of need for achievement were less confirmative. An additional striking result was that the importance scores of the personality traits were not high in most groups of tasks.

The importance of the competencies for performing the roles is presented in Table 2. With regard to the roles, the competencies that might be expected to be important were rated as such. For example, it might be supposed that resoluteness is an important competency for the decision-making role, that creativity is important for the creative role, that group and individual leadership is important for the stimulating-leadership role, that perseverance is important for the directive-leadership role, and that teamwork is important for the assisting role. In accordance with the hypotheses, the stimulative- and directive-leadership roles require competencies related to social skills. All the personality traits were rated as important for performing these roles. This finding suggests that the leadership roles require some competencies that are difficult to train. Interestingly, knowledge was found to be relatively unimportant for these roles.

In order to distinguish work domains where the importance of the competencies differs as much as possible, a series of cluster analyses was performed. Because we wanted to join together the tasks and roles with similar importance profiles, the scores were first standardized within tasks and roles. These standardized scores represent the relative importance of the competencies within each task or role. Next, cluster analyses using the K-means method with

TABLE 1
Importance of Competencies Within Groups of Tasks

Competency	Group of Tasks								
	Data	Func	Faci	Org	Coor	Qual	Proj	Bu	Int
Knowledge:									
Knowledge of IT	■	+	■		■	+		■	
Knowledge of other disciplines				+					+
Knowledge of the environment		+		+	+		+	+	■
Commercial insight									■
Behaviour style:									
Planning and organizing					+		+	+	
Group/individual leadership									
Conflict handling									+
Resoluteness					+	+	+	+	
Convincingness							+		+
Didactic skills									
Initiative					+			+	+
Independence	+	+	+	+	+	+	+	+	+
Communicative skills	+			+	+		+		+
Oral fluency				+	+		+		■
Writing skills				■	+		+		+
Teamwork							+		
Negotiating skills							+		■
Customer orientedness				+			+		■
Working methodically/ accuracy	+	+	+	+	+	+	+	+	+
Listening	+				+	+	+		■
Cognitive capacity:									
Abstraction ability/problem analysis	+	+			+		+	+	
Judgement					+		+	+	+
Creativity	+						+	+	
Analytic ability	■	+	+	+	+		+	+	+
Personality:									
Perseverance							+		+
Flexibility									
Emotional stability/immunity to stress									
Sensitivity									
Need for achievement		+				+	+		
Integrity						+			+
Mean N per group	16.9	21.3	12.2	15.8	14	21.6	21.6	12.7	17.7

Func = functions, Faci = facilities, Org = organization, Coor = coordination, Qual = quality control, Proj = project control, Bu = business management, Int = interaction with environment.
■ = mean score higher than 2.5 (very important), + = mean score between 2 and 2.5 (at least important), no sign = mean score lower than 2 (less important).

TABLE 2
Importance of Competencies for the Performance of Roles

Competency	Roles						
	Deci	*Cons*	*Crea*	*Reco*	*StimL*	*DirL*	*Assis*
Knowledge:							
Knowledge of IT	+	■	+	+		+	+
Knowledge of other disciplines		+	+	+			
Knowledge of the environment	+	+	+	+			
Commercial insight							
Behavioural style:							
Planning and organizing	+				■	+	
Group/individual leaderschip					■	+	
Conflict handling	+				■	■	
Resoluteness	■				+	■	
Convincingness	■	■	+			■	■
Didactic skills		+			+	+	
Initiative		+			+	+	
Independence	+	+	+	+	+	+	+
Communicative skills	■	■	+	+	■	■	+
Oral fluency	+	■	+	+	■	■	+
Writing skills	+	■	+	+	+	+	+
Teamwork					■	+	■
Negotiating skills	+	+			+	+	
Customer orientedness	+	■	+	+	+		
Working methodically/accuracy	+	+		+	+	+	
Listening	+	+	+	+	■	■	+
Cognitive capacity:							
Abstraction ability/problem analysis	+	+	+		+		+
Judgement	■	+	+	+	■	■	
Creativity		+	■	+	+		+
Analytic ability	+		■	+	+	+	+
Personality:							
Perseverance	+	+	+		■	■	+
Flexibility		+	+		■	+	+
Emotional stability/immunity to stress	+				■	■	
Sensitivity	+	+			+	+	
Need for achievement					■	■	+
Integrity	+	+			■	■	
Mean N per group	23	6 1	44	34	25	18	46

Deci = decision-making role, Cons = consultancy role, Crea = creative role, Reco = reconnaisance role, StimL = stimulating-leadership role, DirL = directive-leadership role, Assis = assisting role. ■ = mean score higher than 2.5 (very important), + = mean score between 2 and 2.5 (at least important), no sign = mean score lower than 2 (less important).

Euclidean distances were performed. The analysis with four clusters led to the best interpretable results. Analysis of variance showed that the clusters differed significantly with respect to the importance scores of all the competencies (see Table 3). The cluster membership of the tasks is indicated in the Appendix. The assisting role belongs to the first cluster, the creative role and the reconnaissance roles to the second cluster, the decision-making role, the stimulating-leadership role, and the directive-leadership role to the third cluster, and the advising role to the fourth cluster.

The first cluster is characterized by tasks with a very technical orientation. The inclusion of the assisting role shows that this role requires competencies that are similar to the technical tasks. The cluster centres of this cluster are presented in the second column of Table 3. As might be expected, the competencies of knowledge of information technology and working methodically/accuracy are very important. Analytic ability and independence are also rather important.

The tasks of the second cluster are related to the organization analysis or the adaptation of the system to the specific organization. The reconnaissance role and the creative role are also included in the second cluster. The second cluster may be called the organization-oriented work domain. The most important competencies required in this domain are in descending order: analytic ability, writing skills, judgement, knowledge of the environment, independence, knowledge of information technology, commercial skills, and abstraction ability/problem analysis.

The third cluster consists of three management roles: the decision-making role, the stimulating-leadership role, and the directive-leadership role. This cluster was conceived as the leadership-oriented work domain. In the leadership-oriented work domain, the following competencies are important: resoluteness, convincingness, planning and organizing, communicative skills, oral fluency, independence, initiative, and team work.

The tasks in the fourth cluster are related to the support of end users by means of writing instructions or rendering direct assistance. Because the advisory role was defined as supporting and advising in decision making, it is no surprise that this role also belongs to the fourth cluster. The cluster comprises the user-support oriented work domain. This domain requires the competencies of writing skills, communicative skills, customer orientedness, oral fluency, and listening.

In order to investigate the relationships between the level of work autonomy and the importance of the competencies, the importance scores for the tasks of each subject were averaged. These mean scores were correlated with the level of autonomy as measured with the three-item scale. It was found that autonomy correlated with the importance of the following competencies: convincingness ($r = 0.36$; $P < .01$), oral fluency ($r = 0.30$; $P < .01$), communicative skills ($r = 0.30$; $P < .01$), writing skills ($r = .24$; $P < .05$), and knowledge of other disciplines ($r = 0.23$; $P < .05$). In accordance with previous studies, the results

TABLE 3
Standardized Importance of Competencies Within Competency
Domains and *F*-values

Competency	Cluster				
	1	*2*	*3*	*4*	*F*
Knowledge:					
Knowledge of IT	1.91	0.77	−1.18	0.31	27.6***
Knowledge of other disciplines	−0.46	0.48	−1.50	0.03	27.5***
Knowledge of the environment	−0.04	0.79	−1.06	0.44	25.2***
Commercial insight	−1.65	−1.10	−1.59	−0.73	6.5**
Behavioural style:					
Planning and organizing	0.46	0.07	1.08	−0.83	6.1**
Group/individual leaderschip	−1.31	−1.44	0.53	−1.71	24.7***
Conflict handling	−1.23	−1.28	0.19	−1.10	14.1***
Resoluteness	0.36	0.08	1.32	−0.88	17.6***
Convincingness	−0.52	−0.14	1.21	0.08	17.2***
Didactic skills	−1.02	−1.39	−1.21	0.50	22.1***
Initiative	0.34	0.50	0.72	0.02	2.9*
Independence	0.98	0.79	0.70	0.43	3.9*
Communicative skills	0.33	0.76	0.90	1.39	15.5***
Oral fluency	−0.26	0.29	0.74	1.25	24.3***
Writing skills	0.00	0.91	−0.06	1.46	16.4***
Teamwork	0.35	−0.25	0.67	−0.45	11.4***
Negotiating skills	−0.63	−0.25	0.61	−0.30	7.7***
Customer orientedness	0.00	0.06	−0.53	1.30	16.6***
Working methodically/accuracy	1.56	0.60	−0.30	0.33	46.4***
Listening	0.15	0.54	0.15	0.84	4.3**
Cognitive capacity:					
Abstraction ability/problem analysis	0.29	0.68	−0.89	−0.33	15.4***
Judgement	0.15	0.80	0.55	−0.39	12.0***
Creativity	−0.02	0.22	−0.91	0.08	5.0**
Analytic ability	1.23	1.34	−0.54	0.22	26.4***
Personality:					
Perseverance	−0.06	−0.12	0.58	−0.47	8.2***
Flexibility	−0.14	−0.45	−0.03	0.07	3.7*
Emotional stability/immunity					
to stress	−0.05	−1.10	0.22	−0.57	29.5***
Sensitivity	−0.99	−0.97	−0.59	−0.04	9.2***
Need for achievement	0.25	−0.55	0.32	−0.37	10.7***
Integrity	0.02	−0.62	−0.12	−0.55	7.9***

*$P < .05$, **$P < .01$, ***$P < .001$.

show that the level of autonomy is positively related to the importance of some behavioural characteristics, besides knowledge of other disciplines. Interestingly, all these competencies are related to communication with other people.

DISCUSSION

The results show that four competency domains can be distinguished in business computer science. These competency domains may be described as technique-oriented, organization-oriented, leadership-oriented, and user-support-oriented. These results are useful in the further development of the concept of expertise because they define the domain in which people can be an expert. Usually the domain is the whole job and expertise is based on a composite criterion. However, most jobs consist of several elements that require different competencies. This means that experts in some elements of the job are not necessarily experts in other elements. The necessity for distinguishing work domains is growing because jobs as stable groups of tasks are fading away. As noted before, this is especially true in computer science.

A seemingly contradictory finding is that the agreement of the ratings within groups of tasks was high, while tasks from different groups were grouped in the cluster analysis. This may partly be explained by the standardization of the scores before cluster analysis. Also, the high level of agreement within groups of tasks may result from the fact that some competencies were rated as very important for the performance of most tasks (e.g. knowledge of information technology) and others competencies were mostly rated as not important (e.g. commercial insight). Nevertheless, this result shows that aggregation within the groups was allowed.

Although the present study is based on subjective ratings of the importance of competencies, the results are mainly in accordance with studies using a more objective approach (e.g. Sonnentag, 1995). Nevertheless, the results may have been affected by the fact that the views of other people are not reflected in the data. For example, customers may emphasize the importance of social skills and employees may require more stimulating leadership from their managers.

By relating competencies to tasks and roles and discerning stable and trainable competencies, the results of the study can have an added value for applied human resource management. Organizations may use these results to improve personnel selection through a better specification of the competencies required for the tasks and roles to be accomplished. The competency model for a specific combination of tasks and roles can be derived by simply taking the highest importance of the competencies belonging to these tasks and roles.[1] In addition, the importance of competencies for combinations of tasks and roles may be weighed with the

---

[1]The necessary data for doing so can be obtained from the author.

time spent on these tasks and roles. Srinivasan, Shocker, and Weinstein (1973) described a method for performing this type of weighing. In personnel selection, the stable competencies of applicants should have the level required for the job, but trainable competencies may be somewhat lower, if the person has the opportunity and the ability to improve them.

The results may also be helpful in career counselling. Employees should rate their own competencies on behaviourally anchored rating scales.[2] On the basis of the profile of scores and the wishes of the employee, the competency domain or domains are chosen in which he or she can make a career. In cooperation with the counsellor, the tasks and roles are selected that match the needs of the individual and the organization. If a person lacks some trainable competencies, these should be trained. However, if a person does not have the stable competencies required, a change to the new composition of tasks is not advisable.

Finally, organizations may use the findings for designing a performance appraisal system. On the basis of the tasks and roles performed, the competencies can be selected that are important for high performance. These competencies can be rated on the behaviourally anchored rating scales mentioned earlier. Such an approach to performance appraisal may be used in a competency-based organization as described Lawler (1994).

A limitation of this study is that some tasks were rated by only a small number of subjects. This may cast some doubt on the reliability and representativeness of the importance scores on individual tasks. However, the reliability of the task ratings was quite high. Besides, the main results presented in Tables 1 and 2 are based on the importance of the competencies for several tasks/roles, involving the ratings of a larger group of subjects.

Future studies should investigate the predictive validity of competencies for the performance of tasks and roles in business computer science. For the assessment of multiple criteria, different raters should be used depending on the type of tasks and roles. For example, in the technique-oriented work domain, performance may be rated by the supervisor, in the organization-oriented domain by the client organization, in the leadership-oriented domain by team members and a supervisor, and in the user-support-oriented domain by end users. The practicality of a method based on the assessment of competencies for tasks and roles should also be studied in the context of career counselling, personnel selection, and performance appraisal.

REFERENCES

Barrick, M.R., & Mount, M.K. (1991). The big five personality dimensions and job performance: A meta-analysis. *Personnel Psychology, 44,* 1–24.

Bridges, W. (1994). *Jobshift: How to prosper in a workplace without jobs.* Reading, UK: Addison-Wesley.

---

[2]Such scales are available from the author.

Curtis, B., Krasner, H., & Iscoe, N. (1988). A field study of the software design process for large systems. *Communications of the ACM, 31*, 1268–1287.

Dutch Computer Society. (1993). *Tasks and functions in business informatics: A proposal for classification.* Amsterdam, The Netherlands: Dutch Computer Society.

Ericsson, K.A., & Smith, J. (1991). Prospects and limits of the empirical study of expertise: An introduction. In K.A. Ericsson & J. Smith (Eds), *Toward a general theory of expertise: Prospects and limits* (pp. 1–38). Cambridge, UK: Cambridge University Press.

Eteläpelto, A. (1993). Metacognition and the expertise of computer program comprehension. *Scandinavian Journal of Educational Research, 37*, 243–254.

Guion, R.M. (1965). Synthetic validity in a small company. *Personnel Psychology, 18*, 4–63.

Lawler, E.E. (1994). From job-based to competency-based organizations. *Journal of Organizational Behavior, 15*, 3–15.

Mabe, P.A., & West, S.G. (1982). Validity of self-evaluation of ability: A review and meta-analysis. *Journal of Applied Psychology, 67*, 280–296.

Schmidt, F.L., & Kaplan, L.B. (1971). Composite vs. multiple criteria: A review and solution of the controversy. *Personnel Psychology, 39*, 848–851.

Sonnentag, S. (1995). Excellent software professionals: Experience, work activities, and perceptions by peers. *Behaviour and Information Technology, 14*, 289–299.

Spencer, L.M., & Spencer, S.M. (1993). *Competence at work: Models for superior performance.* New York: John Wiley.

Srinivasan, V., Shocker, A.D., & Weinstein, A.G. (1973). Measurement of a composite criterion of managerial success. *Organizational Behavior and Human Performance, 9*, 147–167.

Van den Berg, P.T., & Feij, J.A. (1993). Personality traits and job characteristics as predictors of job experiences. *European Journal of Personality, 7*, 337–357.

Vessey, I. (1986). Expertise in debugging computer programs: An analysis of the content of verbal protocols. *IEEE Transactions on Systems, Man, and Cybernetics, 16*, 247–278.

Weiser, M., & Shertz, J. (1983). Programming problem representation in novice and expert programmers. *International Journal of Man–Machine Studies, 19*, 391–398.

Zachman, J.A. (1987). A framework for information systems architecture. *IBM Systems Journal, 26*, 276–292.

APPENDIX

Cluster Membership of Tasks in Business Computer Science
(Dutch Computer Society, 1993)

Cluster

Data
2 compose object model
2 compose data model
1 manage meta-data
1 compose implementation data model
1 perform data conversion
4 provide ad hoc information
1 manage data

Functions
2 compose business process model
2 compose information process model
2 select applications packages
2 design functional specifications

Cluster

1 manage parameters
1 design application structure
2 design manual information processes
1 design program specifications
1 make program
1 install applications software
1 manage program libraries

Facilities
1 specify technical infrastructure blueprint
1 quantify information system capacity
1 design computer system configurations
1 design network
1 manage technical infrastructure capacity

Cluster

1   manage data processing components
1   manage data storage components
1   manage network
2   select technical infrastructure components
1   configure technical infrastructure components
1   install technical infrastructure components
1   recover from system breakdowns
1   plan operations
1   operate equipment
1   manage computer usage
1   manage network usage

Organization

2   investigate organizational aspects
2   analyse ability to change
2   organize information management function
4   compile instructions for use
4   compile user manual
4   compile operations manual
1   administer use authorization

Coordination

2   compose information policy
2   determine decision criteria
2   determine information architecture
2   analyse information services
2   determine the desired situation
2   determine alternative solutions
2   specify implementation strategy
2   determine projects for information services
2   specify transition step
2   specify internal audit/security measures
2   monitor information system
2   determine information system architecture
1   specify conversion strategy
1   draw up system test plan

Cluster

1   draw up acceptance test plan
1   determine systems maintenance
1   perform system test
1   carry out acceptance test
1   protect data processing systems
2   evaluate information system
4   provide front line support
4   support personal computing
1   supervise usage

Quality control

1   determine development standards
1   support development standards
1   determine standards for systems operations and control
1   determine operations standards
1   assure quality

Project control

2   explore problems
2   define project assignment
3   formalize project organization
3   start assignment
2   draw up schedule
3   control performance
2   compile report
2   evaluate assignment
4   organize transfer of knowledge
2   define area of investigation
2   perform risk analysis

Business management

2   investigate data processing developments
1   manage changes to technical infrastructure
1   manage problems

Interaction with the environment

2   manage contracts
4   manage customer relations
4   undertake commercial tasks

A Commentary on "Competencies for Work Domains in Business Computer Science" by P.T. van den Berg

Ales Gregar, ZPS a.s., Zlin, Czech Republic

I think that this article presents a very interesting and very stimulating view of the problem of ongoing changes in human resource management—not only in IT jobs. The concept of competencies for work domains, as elements of expertise for performance of tasks and roles, is understandable and good for application to human resource management of modern organizations.

This concept corresponds to today's situation: Employees often change tasks within the same job because they work on temporary projects or work domains. Findings in this article are relevant for human resource oriented management and also be used for personnel selection, personnel training, and personnel consultancy. It opens up possibilities for personnel management which is oriented this way, and can enable people to be more employable in organizations. It helps employees in making career choices. It helps personnel managers to create good professional training programmes for their organizations and to undertake good personnel consultancy for improving their most important competitive advantage—the knowledge, skills, and abilities of their employees. In this context, expertise is potentially a very important concept for each organization.

Relating competencies to tasks and roles and discerning stable and trainable competencies has good value for applied human resource management. It is possible to use it in personnel selection, in better specification of the competencies required for tasks and roles and their potential changes. If a person lacks some trainable competencies, these should be trained. As Van den Berg states: "If a person does not have the stable competencies required, a change to the new composition of tasks is not advisable." This is applicable to career counselling. It is also a good idea to use the findings for designing a performance appraisal system. It is possible to select the competencies that are important for high performance at relevant work domains (tasks and roles).

Finally, I think that Mr van den Berg's article is good work—not only on a "theoretical field" (good theoretical concept and good methodology), but it has also good practical relevance for human resource management (human oriented), and not only in IT jobs. This concept of competencies for work domains can be used within any other business in order to enable better coping with the rapid change in job definition in response to the globalization of the world economy and the world of the work.

EUROPEAN JOURNAL OF WORK AND ORGANIZATIONAL PSYCHOLOGY, 1998, 7 (4), 533–547

Exploring the Nature of Human Resource Developers' Expertise

Tuija Valkeavaara

Institute for Educational Research, University of Jyväskylä, Finland

This article explores the nature of expertise of HR developers who work on training, career development, and developmental processes in an organization. The study draws on the data from a survey on HR developers in Finland ($n = 164$), possessing both quality and length of education and experience typical of experts in HRD. The HR developers evaluated their work performance through work roles and outputs, importance of competencies needed in performance, and related developmental interests in competencies. The results indicated that in terms of work performance there are specific areas of change agency, trainership, and management in HRD work determined mostly by contextual factors; there is also a common element which refers to dealing with the less explicit processes of change. Also, there seem to be common areas in expert knowledge, but the importance of these varies according to work role. In terms of importance and developmental interest, analytical and coaching competence seemed to be central. Seemingly both are less explicit and informal areas of expert knowledge. Additionally, both are acquired mainly through experience, and are areas which enable expertise to be communicated and mediated for the use of the organization. These findings are discussed further in relation to the nature and further development of HR developer's expertise.

Expertise among HR developers has been mentioned as one of the key factors for the effectiveness of the developmental processes in work organizations. It has been suggested as important, especially in those organizations that strive to incorporate human learning into their ongoing production. It is also emphasized in order to meet the challenges for Europe as a collective learning society (Nijhof, 1996). Even though human resource development (HRD) in modern work organizations comprises an extensive applied domain of expertise with a broad variety of underlying theories of work and organizational psychology, as well as theories of learning and adult education and of business and management, it has

Requests for reprints should be addressed to T. Valkeavaara, Institute for Educational Research, Research Group on Learning and the Acquisition of Professional Expertise, University of Jyväskylä/Dept. of Education, PO Box 35, FIN-40351 Jyväskylä, Email: tvalkeav@campus.jyu.fi

The study reported in this article has been funded by the "Impact and Effectiveness of Education" research programme of the Academy of Finland.

been less studied as a specific domain of expertise. HRD means primarily training, career development, and organization development in the work organization. Furthermore, it also includes other organizations' human resource functions with the aims of fostering learning capacity at all levels of an organization, integrating learning culture into overall business strategy, and also striving for high quality performance (Marsick & Watkins, 1992; McLagan, 1996).

HR developers are seen here as practitioners who are engaged in work organizations in the practice of HRD either as full-time or part-time practitioners, or as an external consultants (Nadler & Nadler, 1991). In the broadest sense, HR developers are involved in lifelong learning and the development of adults within various workplace contexts (Marsick & Watkins, 1992). In fact, they can be as much involved or even more so in reflective processing of individuals' tacit knowledge, such as personal beliefs and mental models, in the organization, than in working with more explicit instruments, such as official intentions, technology, and formal knowledge and skills, which create the visible production of the company (Doherty, 1996; Webb, 1995). Consequently, their work can be described as backstaging, as defined by Buchanan and Boddy (1992) as influencing, negotiating, and bargaining in cultural systems between the individuals and the organization.

Recent discussion and studies of European HR developers' work (e.g. Attwell, 1997; Tjepkema & Wognum, 1996; Valkeavaara, 1997) have presented HR developers in the demanding developmental processes as consultants, change agents, or facilitators of learning. However, despite efforts to define and equally to strengthen HRD as a profession and as a special domain of expertise, it can be characterized as "homeless" (Filander, 1997) or rather as a domain with many home bases having no unified theoretical background or well-defined set of duties and requirements. Nevertheless, Hansen, Kahnweiler, and Wilensky (1994) have demonstrated that HR developers seem to share common conceptions of their work in an organization with the focus on people and their development and interpersonal relations. From the HR developers' point of view, the requirements of the present situation may have two sides: on the one hand, they are expected, more than before, to have domain-specific formal knowledge related to learning, training, and organization developmental theories and techniques. On the other hand, the ill-defined and polycontextual situations they face emphasize more general and practical knowledge, which forms the less explicit and less trainable aspects of expertise, for example, self-knowledge and interpersonal skills (Dipboye, 1997).

In order to ensure the development of expertise in HRD and, further, the effectiveness of HRD in an organization, we need to analyse what constitutes expertise in HRD, i.e. what comprises the activities and products of HRD work and the necessary knowledge and skills it involves. Thus, exploring the nature of expertise as it is seen by practising HR developers themselves, may contribute to the development of their expertise as well as to the evaluation of their work in organizations. This may also give guidelines to those in charge of recruiting HRD personnel in organizations. It is also important to explore what kind of role the various knowledge and skills play in HRD expertise, especially the practical and less explicit dimensions. HR developers are constantly working in ill-defined developmental duties and contexts without unified formal qualifications. Accordingly, their expertise and professional status is primarily built on the interaction between the actual demands and the practical implications necessary in order to meet those demands.

How, then, should the nature of expertise in HRD practice be explored? The traditional, cognitive–psychological studies of expertise have focused on structures of formal knowledge that an individual acquires through formal education and practice, develops vertically through different phases of knowledge acquisition, and finally uses for superior performance in well-structured problem situations (Engeström, Engeström, & Kärkkäinen, 1995; Tynjälä, Nuutinen, Eteläpelto, Kirjonen, & Remes, 1997). However, the ill-defined problems with no clear optimal solution which today's work life offers, especially for HR developers, call for an alternative approach to expertise. Thus, this article argues that the nature of workplace expertise can be characterized as suggested by Bereiter and Scardamalia (1993), as an interactive and continuously developing process of performing, based on a combination of both domain-specific and general knowledge, both formal and practical in its nature. In terms of expert knowledge, Bereiter and Scardamalia (1993) describe expertise as composed of a variety of formal knowledge and skills acquired mainly through education and of different forms of less explicated and tacit knowledge, which they term "hidden", learnt through experience. This less explicated knowledge plays an important role in an expert's work. It is actualized and acquired in those everyday activities of apprehending, analysing, communicating, and performing in different formal and informal situations, in making practical and theoretical judgements, and in reflecting personal strategies in performances. Accordingly, the difference between expert and novice is not necessarily only in the length and quality of education and experience (Tynjälä et al., 1997) but also in the ways in which the experience and hidden knowledge it engenders are applied.

Extensive research on HR developers has been carried out especially in the USA (e.g. McLagan, 1989; Nadler & Nadler, 1991), but less so in the European context. That research has focused on work roles and competencies in order to define the field and its standards. It has built our conception of HR developers' manifold work performances through various work roles, especially as trainers but also as managers or consultants. A variety of competencies needed for those performances have been defined, for instance those related to understanding in organization development, human learning, and management as well as skills for organization and communication. Nevertheless, the research which exists has been less concerned with the overall nature of expertise, as is also the case in the vast majority of research on expertise which has focused on the structures of formal knowledge and skills. At the same time there are fewer studies of the less explicit parts of expertise. In terms of those parts of expert knowledge, for instance, psychological, metacognitive, or informal knowledge in various professional practices (e.g. Bullock, James, & Jamieson, 1995; Eteläpelto, 1993; Rambow & Bromme, 1995; Salloum, 1996) have been studied through special tasks, experiences, and conceptions of work and related knowledge and skills. These studies have shown the practical nature of expertise and that usually, the more experience the practitioner has gained, the greater part practical knowledge, i.e. knowledge and skills in decision making, interpersonal relationships, delegation, practical judgements, and metacognitive knowledge have in his or her expertise. Furthermore, in terms of exploring the nature of expertise, seeing expertise as an active process of doing implies the view of work-related knowledge as a process of knowing manifested through human performance (Blackler, 1995). This allows the possibility to explore the nature of expertise by observing performance on the spot but also by asking the practitioners to describe their conceptions of actual performance and activities in their work, i.e. their work role, and the outputs which are produced through the performance (e.g. McLagan, 1989). Accordingly, performance and its products interact with various kinds of competencies, which are potential, both formal and informal knowledge and skills used for the success of performance and upon which expertise is founded (Ellström, 1994). Furthermore, the developmental view of competencies has been rarely connected to the studies of expertise, even though it is embedded in the characterizations of expertise as a continuously developing process. Consequently, developmental interests can be seen to reflect situations from which development of expertise originates.

In sum, by relating a practitioner's conceptions of his or her personal work performance seen through work role and its direct products, the importance of competencies needed for performance, and interests in further development in competencies gives us a holistic description of the structure of expertise in HRD (Hager & Gonczi, 1996). Consequently, the present study sought to explore the nature of those HR developers' expertise practising in Finland through their conceptions of the dimensions mentioned previously. This was achieved by drawing on the results of a survey where the adopted self-evaluative instrument was based on the descriptive model for HRD work by McLagan (1989). The study aimed to answer the following research questions: (1) How do the HR developers' conceptions of their work performance in terms of work roles and outputs differ and how do the conceptions describe their expertise? and (2) What can we say about the underlying structure of expert knowledge and interests in continuous development in expertise on the basis of the evaluation of importance of competencies and interests in personal further development in competencies and how are they related to work performance?

METHOD

Participants

The target group of the study were the HR developers involved in HRD function in different organizations in Finland: 699 HR developers were selected from 2 Finnish associations of human resource development and human resource management and approached for participation in this study. The selection was purposeful, based on information of who had allowed her or his contact address for non-association purposes. The subjects received a questionnaire by mail at the end of 1995 and at the beginning of 1996. Despite reminders and encouragement from the directories of the associations the response rate was eventually 23.5% ($n = 164$). A study of the prevalence of respondents' gender and age indicated that they were representative of the respective Finnish associations. Similarly, a comparison between the response and the non-response group revealed no significant differences in this respect.

As Table 1 shows, the participating HR developers tended to have a fairly long education, professional further education especially linked with HRD, showed involvement in HRD as their career and had long work experience in general and in their current practice. This fulfilled the prerequisites, i.e. length of education and professional experience, set for the high level of expertise in traditional expert research (Tynjälä et al., 1997). Furthermore, long professional experience tends to enable self-regulatory analysis of personal conceptions of work performances (Eteläpelto, 1993). In addition, the diversity of HRD as a profession and domain of expertise can be seen in the variety of disciplines the participants came from and in the diversity of their work titles.

Materials

An established model (McLagan, 1989) for the description of HRD work was further modified and applied as an self-evaluative instrument. In the questionnaire, the HR developers named one role out of eleven possible work roles which best described the performance most central in their work. The role alternatives were: administrator, evaluator, HRD manager, HRD materials developer, career development adviser, instructor/trainer, marketer, needs analyst, organization change agent, programme designer, and researcher. The work role referred to subjective orientation to actual performance, behaviour, and activities associated with work. The participants ($n = 164$) were grouped into four work role groups according to the work role central to their work performance (see Valkeavaara, 1997). The work role groups were formed so as to take into consideration the three most prevalent roles found in this study, namely organization change agent, programme designer, and HRD manager. Another considered aspect in forming the work role groups was the contents of the role descriptions from McLagan's

TABLE 1
Characteristics of the Participants ($n = 164$)

Variable	f	%
Gender		
female	77	47.0
male	87	53.0
Age		
25–34	6	3.7
35–44	38	23.3
45–55	97	59.9
>55	22	13.5
Educational level		
university degree	147	90.3
Field of education		
economics/administrational/law	60	40.0
educational/behavioural/social	67	44.7
natural/technical	23	15.3
Professional further education in HRD		
yes	131	82.9
Years of work experience in general		
5–9	9	5.5
>10	154	94.5
Years of experience in HRD work		
<1–4	10	6.2
5–9	34	21.0
>10	118	72.8
Years of experience in present work		
<1–4	54	33.1
5–9	59	36.2
>10	50	30.7
Future orientation in HRD		
yes	125	79.1
Formal job title		
trainer/teacher/consultant	28	18.3
HRD manager/designer	56	36.6
HRM manager	29	19.0
other manager	40	26.1
% of working time spent in HRD		
<10–24	33	26.9
25–49	24	15.0
50–100	93	58.1
Position in relation to an organization		
internal full-time	77	52.4
internal part-time	33	22.4
external	37	25.2

(1989) study and her suggestion for revision (McLagan, 1996). The group of change agents ($n = 51, 31.1\%$) was a combination of organization change agents and reflective practitioners who were a new, but minor, work role found in the study. Change agents were practitioners who saw themselves performing most often as supporters of organizational changes and development. Designers ($n = 37, 22.6\%$) were all programme designers. Thus, they were practitioners who saw their performance most often characterized by organizing specific HRD interventions. The group of managers ($n = 50, 30.5\%$) was a combination of HRD managers, marketers, administrators, and consultative communicators, another new but minor work role found in the study. Managers were practitioners who spent most of their working time as providers of HRD function in an organization by managing, marketing, administrating the HRD function, and internally consulting in developmental situations. Practitioners who thought that their performance was specialized in actual learning and training processes, that is, needs assessment, material development, instruction, evaluation, coaching, research, or career development as most typical for their work, were termed trainers ($n = 26$, 15.9%). This role group was a combination of needs analysts, researchers, HRD materials developers, instructors/facilitators, career development advisers, evaluators, and coaches. The role of coach was the third new, but of infrequent occurrence, work role for HR developer found in this study.

The HR developers also indicated (yes/no) which of 74 outputs they actually produced in their most central work role. Outputs were seen as the actual products and services generated as direct outcomes of the work role. The work roles together with the outputs were seen here to describe the HR developer's work performance, which is undertaken according to the requirements and aims of the specific work and which may or may not constitute the whole content. The chi-square test revealed significant relationships between the work role groups, and the background variables presented in Table 1, field of education, $G^2 (6, N = 150) = 20.60, P < .01$, formal job title, $G^2 (9, N = 153) = 25.33, P < .01$, amount of working time spent in HRD tasks, $G^2 (6, N = 160) = 15.60, P < .05$, and position in relation to organization, $G^2 (6, N = 147)\ 15.08, P < .05$. This result demonstrates that HR developer's work role is related on the one hand to the person's original theoretical background acquired through formal education. On the other hand, performing in a certain work role is clearly related to contextual factors in the ongoing work in an organization instead of previous experience or further education.

Further, HR developers evaluated 35 different competencies presented in the model according to their importance (a four-point scale from very important, $l = 3$, to not at all important, $l = 0$) as regarded performing in the central work role and by interest in further development in each competency (a four-point scale from very interested, $l = 3$, to not at all interested, $l = 0$). Competencies described the expert knowledge needed in HRD work through a potential of cognitive, affective, and motor skills and factors, personality traits, and social skills, which thus covered both trainable formal knowledge and skills and general, less explicit, knowledge. Importance of competencies referred to subjectively determined knowledge and skills which contribute to the requirements of successful work performance (Ellström, 1994; McLagan, 1989). Evaluation of interest in personal development in competencies referred to areas in which HR developers experience a need for continuous development of their expertise. It was also seen to reflect those areas where HR developers may find themselves working at the limits of their knowledge. The questionnaire was tested by interviewing four HR developers and by a pilot group ($n = 27$) consisting of the participants of a Programme Design Course for HRD practitioners. The questionnaire was also discussed in cooperation with the corresponding HRD research project (e.g. Odenthal & Nijhof, 1996).

An explorative factor analysis (Principal Axis Analysis with varimax rotation) was conducted to reduce the number of competency variables for further analysis and in order to explore the underlying structure of knowledge and skills evaluated by their importance in HRD work.[1] The factor analysis yielded a solution of four dimensions of expert knowledge which explained 44.8% of the variance in total. The first factor was named as Analytical Competence. The marking competencies in this factor were data reduction skill, intellectual versatility, observing skill, industry understanding, and negotiation skill. The second factor was named as Managerial Competence. The marking competencies were electronic systems skills, facilities skills, records management skills, and cost-benefit analysis skills. The third factor was called Coaching Competence, since its marking competencies were the skills of questioning, coaching, performance observation, and feedback. The last factor was named as Developmental Competence, with the marking competencies of organization development theories and techniques understanding, organization behaviour understanding, and training and development theories and techniques understanding. Internal consistencies for factors were, respectively, 0.81, 0.79, 0.77, and 0.74 (alpha). The same structure of factors and combinations of competencies in the factors were used also for describing the developmental interests. Internal consistencies (alpha) for Analytical Interest was 0.87, for Managerial Interest 0.81, for Coaching Interest 0.79, and for Developmental Interest 0.79. The sum variables and means for each competence dimension and interest dimension were used in further analysis.

---

[1]Detailed information about the factor solutions are available from the author on request.

TABLE 2
Summary of the Chi-square Tests of the Differences Between Work Role Groups in the Most Prevalent Work Outputs

Outputs	Work roles										$G^2(3)$
	Change Agents		Designers		Managers		Trainers		Total		
	%	(n)	%	(n)	%	(n)	%	(n)	%	(n)	
Client awareness of relationships within and around the organization[1]	80.0	(45)	75.6	(36)	85.4	(48)	72.0	(25)	79.2	(154)	2.34
Designs for change[1]	91.8	(49)	69.4	(36)	77.3	(44)	87.0	(23)	81.6	(152)	8.23*
Recommendations to management regarding HRD systems[1]	83.7	(49)	72.2	(36)	89.1	(46)	87.5	(24)	83.2	(155)	4.34
Concepts, theories, or models of development or change[1]	81.1	(49)	72.2	(36)	73.9	(46)	88.0	(25)	78.2	(156)	3.15
Sales and business leads[2]	72.3	(47)	34.3	(35)	69.6	(46)	58.3	(24)	60.5	(152)	14.36**
Data analysis and interpretation[2]	84.1	(44)	58.3	(36)	71.1	(45)	64.0	(25)	70.7	(150)	7.30
Resolved conflicts for an organization or groups[2]	73.9	(46)	42.9	(35)	55.8	(43)	54.2	(24)	58.1	(148)	8.52*
Changes in group norms, values, culture[2]	76.6	(47)	47.2	(36)	50.0	(44)	70.8	(24)	60.9	(151)	11.15*
Plans to implement organizational change	87.5	(48)	47.2	(36)	63.6	(44)	65.2	(23)	67.5	(151)	17.00***
Implementation of change strategies[2]	86.4	(44)	52.8	(36)	67.4	(46)	65.2	(23)	69.1	(149)	11.53**
HRD promotional and informational material[3]	46.5	(43)	72.2	(36)	57.4	(47)	60.9	(23)	58.4	(149)	5.50
Plans to market HRD products, services, and programmes[3]	54.8	(42)	75.7	(37)	67.4	(46)	59.1	(22)	64.6	(147)	4.27
Resource acquisition and allocation for HRD[4]	53.3	(45)	48.6	(35)	72.9	(48)	45.5	(22)	57.3	(150)	7.64
HRD department strategy[4]	63.0	(46)	54.3	(35)	75.6	(45)	60.9	(23)	64.4	(149)	4.26
HRD budgets and financial management[4]	42.9	(42)	50.0	(36)	74.5	(47)	54.5	(22)	56.5	(147)	10.33*
Programme/intervention designs[4]	72.7	(44)	66.7	(36)	70.2	(47)	43.5	(23)	66.0	(150)	6.17
Feedback to learners[5]	43.2	(44)	51.4	(35)	47.7	(44)	76.9	(26)	52.3	(149)	8.56*
Facilitation of group discussions[5]	55.6	(45)	40.0	(35)	18.2	(44)	69.2	(26)	43.3	(150)	22.51***
Facilitations of structured learning events[5]	57.8	(45)	60.0	(35)	29.5	(44)	73.1	(26)	52.7	(150)	15.41**

Outputs produced by two-thirds or more in [1]each work role group; [2]only by change agents; [3]only by designers; [4]only by managers; [5]only by trainers. All as percentage of yes answers, according to the cross tabulation prior to chi-square test. $*P < .05$; $**P < .01$; $***P < .001$.

RESULTS

As can be seen in Table 2, the most prevalent outputs in every work role group, apart from "designs for change", were as typical in their work role among all the HR developers regardless of their perceived work role. This result demonstrates that the general part of performing in the work role in terms of outputs is oriented to change, development, negotiating, and seeking support for the HRD function in an organization. Further, it implies that the general element in HR developers' expertise is connected with less explicit information services and analyses of symbols which are actualized in practice at the implicit level of organizational processes rather than with concrete and countable products.

The statistical differences between the work role groups in outputs are also presented in Table 2. The differences suggest that change agents and trainers constitute two specific groups among HR developers. The specific outputs of change agents and trainers referred clearly to situations where they have to facilitate change and learning, ask questions, make interpretations, and give judgements related to less explicit aspects of developmental processes. For change agents this seemed to be based not only on the immediate situation but also on the long-term goals of an organization, while for trainers the emphasis was on the present learning event. Consequently, these results refer to adaptation of informal and less explicit knowledge rather than the deliberate use of certain formal techniques. Further, the outputs which were most prevalent among designers and managers demonstrated that their work role was focused more on concrete products which maintain HRD function, including marketing plans and materials, intervention designs, strategy statements, and budgets. Accordingly, this refers to use of specific knowledge on design and management.

As can be seen from Table 3, analytical and coaching competences were evaluated as the most important dimensions of expert knowledge among the HR developers. In these dimensions, HR developers were also the most interested in developing themselves. The importance of analytical competence referred to intellectual and thinking skills but also to communication skills which will enable the HR developer to make use of knowledge that has been acquired and observed. This result suggests the centrality of both processing and using knowledge in interpersonal relations and across the different situations in HRD work. Coaching competence and a related developmental interest in it indicated the importance of skills in observing and identifying the situation, giving feedback, and coaching groups and individuals. In terms of interests these results suggest that, in general, situations where the HR developers work at the limits of their knowledge and skills deal with organizational communication, use of knowledge, and coaching.

As shown in Table 3, on the one hand the type of work role produced certain differences in how the various dimensions of expert knowledge were evaluated. On the other hand, the results showed that to a large extent the dimensions of

TABLE 3
Summary of One-way Analyses of Variance for Work Role Groups and Dimensions of Expert Knowledge and Interests in Personal Further Development

| | Work Roles | | | | | | | | | |
| | Change Agents | | Designers | | Managers | | Trainers | | | |
	M	SD	M	SD	M	SD	M	SD	n	F(df)
Dimensions of expert knowledge:										
1 Analytical competence	2.51	0.40	2.48	0.43	2.40	0.51	2.54	0.37	160	0.80 (3, 156)
2 Managerial competence	1.95	0.48	1.92	0.41	2.03	0.45	2.02	0.52	160	0.53 (3, 156)
3 Coaching competence	2.33	0.46	2.30	0.41	2.28	0.47	2.58	0.32	160	2.87 (3, 156)*
4 Developmental competence	2.34*	0.41	2.11	0.52	2.06*	0.53	2.28	0.48	159	3.38 (3, 155)*
Interests in further development:										
1 Analytical interest	2.22	0.60	2.27	0.52	2.21	0.60	2.43	0.41	159	1.07 (3, 155)
2 Managerial interest	1.87	0.60	1.76	0.44	1.97	0.49	1.98	0.49	159	1.34 (3, 155)
3 Coaching interest	2.13	0.63	2.19	0.42	2.15	0.48	2.36	0.46	159	1.21 (3, 155)
4 Developmental interest	2.21	0.49	1.96	0.59	1.96	0.60	2.17	0.50	158	2.43 (3, 154)

Post-hoc test Sheffe test with significance level 0.05, *P <.05.

expert knowledge and interests were general, as important regardless of the work role. In terms of importance, analytical and managerial competences were the general dimensions of expertise. Their importance was equal in different groups and thus independent from the nature of performing in a certain work role. The differences in work role groups showed that importance of coaching and developmental competences varied according to work role. This result demonstrates how the centrality of actual training, development, and change processes in work role is related to the importance of specific knowledge and skills in expertise.

DISCUSSION

Experts' own conceptions of their personal work role and outputs, importance of competencies needed in performing in the certain work role, and developmental interests in competencies are features seldom studied in research on professional expertise. The present study concentrated on exploring these features of expertise among HR developers. Seen through the work roles and outputs it seems, on the one hand that there are areas of specialization as change agency, trainership, and management within HRD expertise. These fields are determined to a large extent by contextual factors. In these specific areas of activity, the outputs are also answers to special needs. On the other hand, it is likely that working in one specific area only is not enough for the effectiveness of HRD (cf. McLagan, 1989). In this regard the HR developer is expected to cross the boundaries of the work role and to take responsibility for change processes, managerial issues, or the practical arrangements of training in a flexible way. However, as the common work outputs in data showed, there is also a common element in HR developers' work. This means that much of the HR developer's work seems to be responding to ill-defined problems at the more or less tacit levels of organizational activity. They do it by producing information analyses, evaluations, recommendations, and plans rather than delivering concrete products. Consequently, this suggests that there is no unanimous description of an HR developer's expert role but a certain common conception and many situation-dependent alternatives. This shows that HR developers can be termed experts who eventually build their own role in organizational settings (Attwell, 1997).

The different competence dimensions in expert knowledge, in general, correspond to earlier conceptions of HRD work. However, the centrality and importance of analytical and coaching competences compared to others suggests that the type of expertise described by Bereiter and Scardamalia (1993) as consisting of asking the right questions and using knowledge creatively is an especially important area in HRD work. It also suggests that HR developers have to be able to communicate and mediate their expertise for the use of the other people in the organization, mainly through language and collaboration (Bereiter & Scardamalia, 1993; Blacker, 1995). In other words, it is not enough for an HR developer to know the organizational theories or training techniques; these also have to be made available for people within the organization. Further, these competences refer to obviously hidden areas of expert knowledge which are acquired through experience rather than theoretical studies. In all, the results suggest that the core of expertise lies in knowing developmental processes in organizational settings instead of knowing thoroughly the technical aspects of organization-specific production. Consequently, the questions which have to be considered are: where to place the focus in the education and recruitment of HR developers, how to make hidden knowledge more explicit, how to evaluate the effectiveness of HR developers who seem to act in the implicit processes of an organization, and how to build education that provides experiences for the construction of the hidden knowledge.

The results also indicated that there are general, both less explicit and formal dimensions of expert knowledge of equal importance, regardless of performance. But, there are competence dimensions which are more important in some specific work roles and also involve both kinds of expert knowledge. Consequently, it is likely that if an HR developer has to cross over the boundaries between different types of performing in various work roles, the same flexibility is required from expert knowledge. This also suggests that there is no static description of what is an overall definition of expert knowledge in HRD; it has to interact with the characteristics of work role and, further, with the demands of the work. Furthermore, the overall developmental interests in competence dimensions supports the idea that HR developers see different evolving areas in their expertise (Blackler, 1995). Thus, for them, expertise is not static nor is it a magical and innate personality-dependent talent which could not otherwise be intentionally developed and learnt (Marsick & Watkins, 1990).

One question that has to be asked is whether the HR developers studied here are actually experts. As noted, in the terms of the criteria used in traditional expert-novice comparisons (Tynjälä et al., 1997) they are all well educated and experienced. But whether they act in the manner of continuously developing and interactive experts in reality is more difficult to judge on the basis of this study. Nevertheless, as argued by Engeström et al. (1995) we should adopt a horizontal and multidimensional approach when defining who is an expert in working life. Thus, merely the ability to communicate one's knowledge to others can make an expert. This was seen as an important area of competence also among the HR developers studied here. Furthermore, using a structured questionnaire with experts who work in open and ill-defined situations, and attempting to divide expertise into competencies may show a certain discrepancy between the theory and the method. Further, it may have reduced the motivation to respond. Also, the hidden expert knowledge is particularly difficult to verbalize through the means of a questionnaire. Nevertheless, during the interviews made later among the same HR developers, they responded that the structured questionnaire gave form to the evaluation of their unstructured work.

Finally, despite the limitations in procedure, the present study as the first phase of a larger research effort on the nature and development of expertise in HRD, succeeded in describing the typical features of expertise among the HR developers. As expertise is seen as an evolving process, the results presented here are bound to a given time and place and should serve as an incentive to further study. They can also give guidelines for the development of the HR developers. The centrality of hidden knowledge in HR developers' expertise makes it especially interesting to direct further study towards how expertise is developed and constructed through experiences in daily work. Also, in terms of the effectiveness of HR developer's work, the focus of research should be moved from definitions and structures to processes, i.e. to the results and manner of how the results are aqcuired in HRD work and how these practitioners actually construct their role and expertise as HR developers.

REFERENCES

Attwell, G. (1997). Pressures for change in the education of vocational education and training professionals. In A. Brown (Ed.), *Promoting vocational education and training: European perspectives* (pp. 107–122). Hämeenlinna, Finland: University of Tampere.

Bereiter, C., & Scardamalia, M. (1993). *Surpassing ourselves: An inquiry into the nature and implications of expertise*. IL: Open Court.

Blackler, F. (1995). Knowledge, knowledge work and organizations: An overview and interpretation. *Organization Studies, 16*, 1021–1046.

Buchanan, D., & Boddy, D. (1992). *The expertise of the change agent: Public performance and backstage activity*. Hemel Hempstead, UK: Prentice Hall.

Bullock, K., James, C., & Jamieson, I. (1995). An exploratory study of novices and experts in educational management. *Educational Management and Administration, 23*(3), 197–205.

Dipboye, R.L. (1997). Organizational barriers to implementing a rational model of training. In M. Quinones & A. Ehrenstein (Eds), *Training for a rapidly changing workplace* (pp. 31–60). Washington: APA.

Doherty, N. (1996). Surviving in an era of insecurity. *European Journal of Work and Organizational Psychology, 5*, 471–478.

Ellström, P.-E. (1994). *Kompetens, utbilding och lärände i arbetslivet* [Competence, training and learning in working life]. Stockholm: Fritzes.

Engeström, Y., Engeström, R., & Kärkkäinen, M. (1995). Polycontextuality and boundary crossing in expert cognition: Learning and problem solving in complex work activities. *Learning and Instruction, 5*, 319–336.

Eteläpelto, A. (1993). Metacognition and the expertise of computer program comprehension. *Scandinavian Journal of Educational Research, 37*, 243–254.

Filander, K. (1997). Kehittäjät tulevaisuuden verkostoasiantuntijoina [Human resource developers as the network experts of the future]. In J. Kirjonen, P. Remes, & A. Eteläpelto (Eds), *Muuttuva asiantuntijuus* (pp. 136–148). Jyväskylä, Finland: University of Jyväskylä, Institute for Educational Research.

Hager, P., & Gonczi, A. (1996). Professions and competencies. In R. Edwards, A. Hanson, P. Raggat (Eds), *Boundaries of adult learning* (pp. 246–260). London: Routledge.

Hansen, C.D., Kahnweiler, W.M., & Wilensky, A.S. (1994). Human resource development as an occupational culture through organizational stories. *Human Resource Development Quarterly, 5*, 253–267.

Marsick, V., & Watkins, K. (1990). *Informal and incidental learning in the workplace*. London: Routledge.
Marsick, V., & Watkins, K. (1992). Building the learning organisation: A new role for human resource developers. *Studies in Continuing Education, 14*(2), 115–129.
McLagan, P. (1989). *Models for HRD practice*. Alexandria: American Society for Training and Development.
McLagan, P. (1996). Great ideas revisited. *Training and Development Journal, 20*(1), 60–65.
Nadler, L., & Nadler, Z. (1991). *Developing human resources* (2nd ed.). San Francisco: Jossey-Bass.
Nijhof, W. (1996). Towards the learning society: Teaching and learning in the European year of lifelong learning. *Lifelong Learning in Europe, 1*(1), 46–50.
Odenthal, L., & Nijhof, W. (1996). *HRD roles in Germany*. De Lier, The Netherlands: Academisch Boeken Centrum.
Rambow, R., & Bromme, R. (1995). Implicit psychological concepts in architects' knowledge—how large is a large room? *Learning and Instruction, 5*, 337–355.
Salloum, K. (1996). The nature of implicit knowledge of senior school administrators: Five vignettes. *Educational Management and Administration, 24*, 425–434.
Tjekpema, S., & Wognum, I. (1996, May). *From trainer to consultant?* Paper presented at the conference of the European Consortium for the Learning Organisation, Copenhagen, Denmark.
Tynjälä, P., Nuutinen, A., Eteläpeito, A., Kirjonen, J., & Remes, P. (1997). The acquisition of professional expertise—a challenge for educational research. *Scandinavian Journal of Educational Research, 41*, 475–494.
Valkeavaara, T. (1997). HRD practitioners analysing their work: What does it tell about their present role in working life? In P. Remes, S. Tøsse, P. Falkenkrone, & B. Bergstedt (Eds), *Social change and adult education research: Adult education research in Nordic countries, 1996* (pp. 14–40). Jyväskylä, Finland: University of Jyväskylä, Institute for Educational Research.
Webb, G. (1995). Reflective practice, staff development and understanding. *Studies in Continuing Education, 17*(1, 2), 70–77.

A Commentary on "Exploring the Nature of Human Resource Developers' Expertise" by T. Valkeavaara

Jim Dukes, Oxford, UK

Well within living memory, professional people joining an organization faced a long and slow climb up a hierarchy. Essential requirements were patience, application, and, above all, deference to the wisdom of one's seniors. Within the last decades this has changed dramatically. Partly this has been the result of the explosion of information technology which meant that senior people—unable or unwilling to learn the necessary skills—were often wholly reliant on the skills and judgement of people much younger than themselves. Further, business schools have increasingly taught techniques designed to replace expert judgement. For these and other reasons, there has been a great loss of respect for wisdom and authority and a greater use of ready-made techniques. There are those who claim that the process has gone too far. They claim that, for example, in Britain the forcing of bank managers into early retirement and replacing their functions by specialists has not been successful.

This paper offers evidence in place of clashing opinions. Critics might argue that the respondents' view that experience is vital is no more than one would expect from any professional group threatened with replacement by systems. Systems, however, require clearly defined situations and, as the author points out, professionals in HR deal largely with situations that are poorly defined. Here formal training is of limited value as it necessarily uses model situations that are clearly defined. This is true even of the most realistic case studies. In real life the situation is nearly always untidy and the practitioner has to deal with the interactions of a large number of interacting variables, rather than a few well-understood effects.

For this reason, people emerging from business schools—here even the most realistic case studies are a simplification of real life—go through a period of adjustment as they learn to adapt theory to practice. Forcing a real-life situation into the shape of a ready-made model can lead to serious trouble. Rather, creative thinking and insight is needed to match models and concepts to the demand of the particular situation. Judgement—of what will work and what will not, of what people will accept or reject—is a vital requirement for HR professionals and only experience can develop it.

There are some questions one would like to ask about the research presented here. Does respect for experience correlate with age? Do the younger respondents have different views?

However, the greater value lies in its bearing on the conflicting claims made for technique and experience and the role of academic study. Practitioners must be equipped with the necessary concepts and models to analyse the situations they come across. But how are they to learn the limitations of these; when and how far to apply them and when to rely on their own judgement? What is the optimum blend of mind-enriching teaching and immediate practical experience and how is it to be achieved?

As the author observes, further research is needed to clarify these vital issues. Meanwhile if the paper prompts us practitioners to re-examine our own experience, it will have a value well beyond its immediate findings.

The author's email address is: jad@dukesja.demon.co.uk

EUROPEAN JOURNAL OF WORK AND ORGANIZATIONAL PSYCHOLOGY, 1998, 7 (4), 549–557

Reaching Business Excellence Through Sound People Management

Susanne Göbel-Kobialka

Siemens Nixdorf Informationssysteme AG, Munich, Germany

Nowadays companies have to cope not only with the increase of knowledge and complexity, but also with continuous change outside and inside the organization. Thus, sound people management is required. During the last couple of years the staff function "Personnel and Organizational Development" of Siemens Nixdorf Informationssysteme AG has developed a modular concept encouraging personal and organizational development. The article outlines the essential elements of the concept (e.g. skills model, staff dialogue MAGplus) pointing out the process of identifying and developing high potentials.

INTRODUCTION

We are the European partner of choice among world-class information technology players. We intend to gain a position of leadership and earn a profit in all segments in which we do business. ... We will achieve excellence through our professionalism and personal skills, which we will continuously develop.

from vision and mission statements of
Siemens Nixdorf Informationssysteme AG

As Siemens Nixdorf Informationssysteme AG (SNI) is part of the growing and very dynamic information technology and service-oriented business, the company has to cope not only with the increase of knowledge and complexity, but also with continuous change outside and inside the organization. Thus open-minded and motivated people with appropriate skills to deal with complexity and change are needed. Moreover, there is the necessity to create a surrounding of a so-called "learning organization", preparing to achieve new business opportunities.

This indicates that reaching business excellence requires sound people management. It is the task of the staff function "Personnel and Organizational Development" (POE) to support business by creating a system to identify and

Requests for reprints should be addressed to S. Göbel-Kobialka, Siemens AG, ICN Ref Pers 7, Hofmannstrasse 51, D-81359 München, Germany.

develop people, especially "high potentials", and providing tools, which encourage personal and organizational development.

Hereafter the modular system of personal and organizational development based on the skills model as a "nucleus" is described. In addition, it will be shown how and to what extent the tools can be used to identify and develop high potentials.

OUTLINE OF THE PERSONNEL DEVELOPMENT CONCEPT

The following list shows the major elements of the personnel development concept introduced at SNI.

- job profiles
- career models
- skills database
- assessment and feedback procedures
- database of high potentials (DIPS)
- human resources market (HRM)

Job Profiles.   These represent a structured and systematic description of the knowledge, experiences, and competencies for specific tasks and functions. The objectives of the job, the lines of communication, the areas and circuit of responsibilities, and the skills required to carry out the tasks are outlined in the job profiles. Thus job profiles ensure clarification of requirements.

Career Models.   These describe functions and possible development paths for each professional area as well as for each business unit. The career model makes evident to every employee the kind and number of development steps they have to pass and the requirements they must fulfil to reach the position they desire. There are three types of career models:

- line management career model
- project management career model
- specialists career model.

Skills Database.   This is the electronic storage of data regarding knowledge, experiences and competencies of all participating employees. Everyone decides if he or she wants to store their skills data. With storing the skills data, they present themselves to an internal job market. By comparing available know-how with market and customer requirements, specific assignments of personnel to particular positions are possible. With this instrument a project manager is able to identify for example the SAP R/3-software specialists he or she needs and could ask them to join the project.

Currently all employees have access to the skills database. An overall mean of 6.94% of the employees has already used the skills database to store their data. The use of the database varies extremely from business unit to business unit. Units with a high portion of work in projects (e.g. solution- and consulting-oriented business units) show a distinctly higher percentage of use than units with a lower number of projects (e.g. product-oriented business units).

Looking at the skills model, the important innovation and difference compared to existing models is the reflection not only on knowledge and professional experience, but also on competencies. The example of skills for commercial management given in Box 1 may illustrate the comprehensive approach.

Assessment and Feedback Procedures. With the staff dialogue (MAGplus) as key instrument, these are the basis for personal and organizational development. The appraisal of the employee's current profile and job performance in the course of an open and honest dialogue constitutes the corporate culture and leads to a learning organization.

The DIPS Database. This provides access to electronic information concerning development potentials and likely job candidates. DIPS holds data of high potentials identified through at least one of the assessment and feedback procedures. It allows a prompt analysis of candidates for key positions—information needed by Human Resources to consult managers properly.

The Human Resources Market (HRM). This contains descriptions of jobs offered within SNI world-wide. The idea of HRM is to create transparency and encourage world-wide job rotations. HRM is an electronic database every employee has access to.

Just to mention it: The electronically based instruments as skill and DIPS database as well as HRM are obviously agreed upon with the works council.

IDENTIFYING HIGH POTENTIALS

There are several tools currently used to identify high potentials Fig. 1).

Staff Dialogue MAGplus

The new staff dialogue MAGplus introduced in 1997 was developed with the support of the university of Trier (group of Dr F.E. Heil). The staff dialogue is based on the skills model—developed together with the university of Trier— and characterized by switching the initiative over to the people. That means it is the responsibility of each employee to care for his or her development and to ensure their own employability. The task of the company according to its understanding is to offer support to help people to develop themselves.

BOX 1
Skills Profile for Commercial Management

Knowledge:
- higher education, college;
- very good knowledge of national industry;
- good knowledge of SNI's product range;
- extensive knowledge of market, trends, and background in the IT market;
- extensive knowledge of all business management processes;
- ability to communicate in English (oral and written).

Experience:
- independent implementation of special tasks and projects;
- supervision, implementation, and commercial control of customer projects;
- minimum of four years in commercial functions, in line management, or staff function;
- three to five years of leadership experience with at least five staff members;
- temporary project work abroad.

General work competence:
- highly advanced analytical thinking and decision making;
- high planning and organizational skills;
- presentation skills;
- good written expression.

Personal work style:
- good ability to handle stress;
- meticulousness;
- marked creativity;
- marked initiative;
- marked achievement orientation.

Communication and cooperation:
- good personal appearance;
- extremely marked self-assertion;
- good ability to cope with conflicts;
- ability to work in a team;
- marked customer-orientation.

Leadership skills:
- marked co-orientation ability;
- marked ability to motivate employees;
- marked ability to delegate;
- marked ability concerning control and supervision;
- marked ability to coach.

Entrepreneurial skills:
- extremely marked entrepreneurial thinking;
- marked orientation toward company and future;
- extremely marked integrity and loyality.

The staff dialogue provides a structure for preparing and carrying out the dialogue between manager and employee. They talk about how objectives of the last period were achieved, which strengths of the person were helpful, which weaknesses have become obvious, and to what extent the behaviour of the

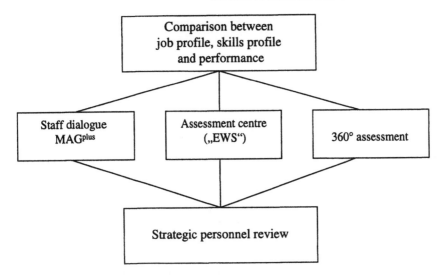

FIG. 1.   Ways of identifying high potentials at SNI.

manager was supporting the achievement of goals. The next step is to discuss and agree upon objectives for the subsequent period. Objectives are not only business goals but also skills-oriented goals, as well as goals for optimizing future cooperation. The agreement also includes planning on further professional development and necessary training measures. For the sake of an open development oriented dialogue, it is important that MAGplus is free from discussion of salary. In addition, manager and employee talk about the potential and possible development steps of the person which are reasonable according to the outlined career model.

So far this is a new element compared to the former staff dialogue as it clarifies the manager's appraisal of the employee. There is no longer something like a hidden appraisal or "secret hit list" of high potentials. This is a milestone on the way to an open, confidence-oriented, learning organization.

It is recommended that the staff dialogue should take place at least once a year. In the year since MAGplus was introduced, no systematic evaluation has yet taken place. Therefore, only some isolated experiences and reactions can be pointed out. The fact that there is a guideline structuring the appraisal as well as the dialogue between employee and manager is one advantage. Another highly appreciated advantage is the use of the skills model which refers not only to knowledge and professional experience, but also highlights the importance of personal competencies in achieving excellent job performance. However, there is one major drawback: The effort of preparing, carrying out and documenting is very high, with a minimum of two–three hours for each person, employee and manager. In some cases this has a negative impact on people's motivation to carry out the MAGplus.

In the meantime the implementation has spread out to the international regions. By the summer of 1997 the implementation had started in Asia Pacific. They now use the tools with slight changes and adaptations to fit with local culture.

Strategic Personnel Review

The statements made in the staff dialogue are used to identify high potentials at the outset. The information will be cross-checked in discussions with managers of the business unit during the yearly "strategic personnel review". Another part of this review is the succession planning for key functions of each business unit. As a result of analysing the information laid down in documentation of staff dialogues and strategic personnel reviews, POE will be able to create a list of high potentials.

Further information could be taken from assessment centres and 360° assessments.

Assessment Centre. There is one type of assessment centres used to identify high potential junior staff of all functional areas. It is the so called "EWS" (development workshop). The participants have some years of professional experience and are about 30 years old. The assessors are top managers, Human Resources people, and at least one psychologist.

The objectives of the EWS are confirming appraisals of superiors as documented in staff dialogues, identifying high potentials in order to start development activities, as well as gathering more detailed information for succession planning. The major intention of the EWS is to support development. Therefore, the individual is provided with a systematic and frank feedback for their personal and professional development.

Methods used at EWS are those known from typical assessment centres such as presentation, group discussions, organizational and planning exercises, etc.

360° Assessment. This kind of assessment offers a complete picture of feedback from all major internal business partners, and is compared with a self-assessment of the manager. The feedback is given through answering a questionnaire which is analysed from an external institute. Employees, co-workers, and the superior of the manager assess the person with the same questionnaire the manager uses for his or her self-assessment. The main objective of this method is to give advice to the manager for personal and professional development.

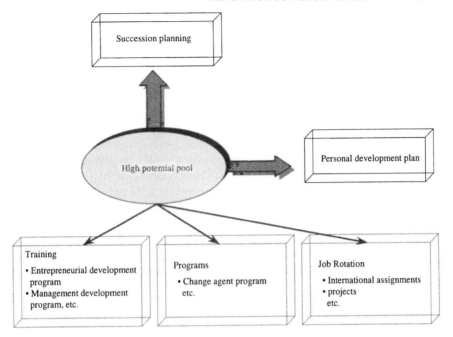

FIG. 2.   Measures developing high potentials at SNI.

DEVELOPING HIGH POTENTIAL

By the time the comparison between job profile and skills profile is finished, measures are defined by the employee and the manager and/or Human Resources. Figure 2 shows examples of possible measures.

Training

Training off the job is one classical method of personnel development. The Entrepreneurial Development Programme (EDP) combines a training off the job with a project in order to develop real entrepreneurial skills. There are two sessions of two weeks duration, and another week of lectures, exercises, and role plays. Additionally, the participants get the instruction to create a business idea, to present the idea to a committee convincing them in order to find a sponsor. The target group of this programme are (top) managers with several years of professional experience.

A shortened version of EDP is the Management Development Programme (MDP). It lasts only one week and there is no project to work on. Target groups for this programme are junior staff and middle management.

Programmes

Another measure is the so-called Change Agent Programme (CAP). Participants of this programme are exempted from their job for one year. During this time they attend lectures in the USA and work on a project to solve an important business problem or to exploit new business opportunities.

Job Rotation

Assignment to a foreign country for one or more years is another kind of measure for developing people. The starting point for an assignment is usually professional know-how in respect of a need for professional support in a foreign country. However, competencies regarding personal work style, communication, co-operation, etc., as the family situation should be taken into consideration. Surveys show that careful selection and preparation is important to ensure successful assignments.

POE has developed an interview guideline to check these critical success factors in advance. The guideline contains questions regarding:

- personal environment (e.g. partner, children, housing);
- environment home country (e.g. network, support for assignment);
- environment host country (e.g. realistic expectations regarding living conditions, information regarding tasks);
- motivation for assignment;
- professional and personal experience (e.g. international experience, language, management experience);
- personal attitude (e.g. ability to handle ambiguous situations, to handle stress, respect for other people).

Checking these criteria as well as using a shortened version of the MAGplus during the assignment are measures that are going to be introduced world-wide. The objectives of these measures are not only to assign the right people and to collect data for personnel development, especially from high potentials, but also to ensure a systematic transfer of knowledge within the company.

SUMMARY

Surviving, or rather excelling, in a rapidly changing and increasingly knowledge-driven business environment requires a very professional, flexible and independent staff. Therefore, a company needs a transparent system to identify and develop such people. At the same time the system should, rather than have people thinking that they are being developed by the company, instead encourage them to ensure their own future employability.

The personnel development concept implemented at SNI provides a consistent and flexible system. With the skills model as basis and centre of the concept the key competencies necessary to cope with change and knowledge increase are emphasized. These competencies are the subject of regular assessments (e.g. as part of the staff dialogue), which also demonstrate their importance to the employees.

Moreover the skills-based approach allows easy adaptations to new requirements. The introduction of the system in the Asia Pacific region has shown that an adaptation to other cultural standards is also feasible.

As the main modules of the system were introduced in 1997, impressive statistics of success can not be presented yet. Nevertheless, we are convinced that we are on the right track with a consistent and transparent system.

A Commentary on "Reaching Business Excellence Through Sound People-Management" by S. Göbel-Kobialka

Tony Keenan, Heriot-Watt University, Edinburgh, UK

This is an interesting report on a system which has been adopted by a particular organization to tackle one of the major HR problems facing many organizations in the late 1990s. Namely, how do you identify and nurture high potential and develop managers in a era where career advancement opportunities are limited and guaranteed employment is a thing of the past?

The first thing that strikes the reader from the perspective of an academic researcher is the fact that, because the system has only been in place for a short period, no data seem to be available as yet on its effectiveness, either as a whole, or in terms of its component parts.

Nowadays, conventional wisdom suggests that HR processes and procedures are built on a foundation of competency analysis. However, although mention is made of the notion of competencies, it is not clear whether a systematic competency analysis was undertaken at the outset of this project and, if so, how this influenced its design and execution.

The idea of a skills database which anyone can sign up for on a voluntary basis is an innovative one. From the point of view of an academic, an interesting question is how well this works in practice. For example, how useful have those seeking jobs and those seeking to fill vacancies found it in practice? The same question could be asked about the database of high potentials described elsewhere in this article.

It is a little surprising that the designers of the system seem to have opted for a fairly conventional appraisal system supplemented by an assessment centre, rather than a more comprehensive performance management approach. In the light of this it would be interesting to know what steps they have taken to overcome the many well-known pitfalls of appraisal systems. Furthermore, although it is an issue which has not received much attention from academic researchers, it seems likely that the adoption of assessment centres as development, rather than selection, tools is much less straightforward that it might appear at first sight. For example, from a motivational point of view, how do you deal with the win/lose psychology development centres create? After all, if some managers are identified as having high potential, others must be labelled as having low potential and this presumably has adverse effects on the level of commitment of the latter group.

In summary, the techniques described in this article are a mixture of innovative ideas and more conventional approaches. Until the system has been running for a longer period and empirical data have been collected and analysed in a systematic manner, from an academic perspective at least, we cannot yet draw any hard and fast conclusions about its efficacy or otherwise.

Training Supervisors' Assessment Skills— A Crucial Step in High Potential Selection

Sabine Remdisch

University of Amsterdam, The Netherlands

Sabine Dionisius

Adam Opel AG, Germany

The example of the Opel high potential selection process indicates that special training programmes that clarify the role and the tasks of supervisors within the selection process are worthwhile. These training programmes help to familiarize supervisors with the standardized assessment forms used in the selection process and to improve their assessment skills. A pilot study with a new training programme showed positive effects. The training ensured high transparency of the whole high potential selection process. The supervisors reported that the training programme had made them more sensitive to the issues of personnel selection and personnel development. On the whole, the quality of the high potential selection process and the accuracy of the assessments could be increased. Furthermore, when supervisory training was completed, supervisors were able to give more detailed and structured feedback information to their employees about their performance behaviour.

INTRODUCTION

The changing nature of work, new concepts of work organization such as group work, global competitive challenges, and ever-present change, require new leadership practices and appropriate managerial skills. Organizations today must have competent managers in order to cope with many complex problems. How can the talent, the potential, required of a competent manager be detected, developed, and measured effectively?

It is important for an organization to identify high potential employees at a very early stage in order to develop them accordingly. More and more organizations become aware of the need and the value of "growing their own". Any process that increases the capabilities and potential of the employees has long-term value and helps the organization to cope with future challenges.

Requests for reprints should be addressed to S. Remdisch and S. Dionisius, Adam Opel AG., Dept. of Organizational Development, ZTOE-76/02, D-65423 Rüsselsheim, Germany; Email: Sabine.Remdisch@psychol.uni-giessen.de

Recently the automobile company Opel (General Motors) applied a highly structured and standardized assessment, selection, and nomination process for high potential employees, as a pilot programme in the German plant at Rüsselsheim. The pilot programme clearly defined roles and responsibilities of the employees, their direct supervisor, and the Human Resource Management (HRM) committee. All supervisors were required to participate in a special training programme before they are allowed to take on an active role in the high potential selection procedure. The training programme clarified the role and the tasks of the supervisors within the selection process and helped to familiarize them with the standardized assessment forms and tools required in the assessment process.

This article concentrates on the role of the supervisors within the high potential selection process. It describes and evaluates the supervisor training programme.

The first section gives an overview of the different steps in the high potential nomination process at Opel. The second section describes the company-specific core competencies used as the basic selection criteria for the high potential employees. The third and fourth sections present the training programme and report the experiences of the supervisors with the training programme.

THE HIGH POTENTIAL SELECTION AND NOMINATION PROCESS AT OPEL

At Opel high potentials are assumed to be young employees that score high on the eight company-specific core competencies and have a substantial number of accomplishments. These accomplishments are defined as having participated in crucial projects—in a leading or major position within the project.

Once a year the Human Resource Management Department approaches all employees with a university degree under the age of 34 for the high potential screening procedure. This includes employees in various departments such as finance, manufacturing, and personnel. Once the employees have declared their commitment for assessment, their direct supervisors are informed by the HRM Department and asked to give their performance evaluation and potential assessment for the candidate. The assessing is done on the basis of three standardized assessment forms: the core competencies profile form, the form for the description of accomplishments, and the final recommendation and decision form. In the next step the supervisors discuss their decision with the head of the department at the next hierarchical level. The high potential selection process finally ends with the HRM committee nominating the best candidates for the high potential development programme. All nominated candidates participate in an Assessment Centre carried out by an independent consulting firm. Those candidates that have presented themselves well are definitely admitted to the development programme (for an overview of the process see Fig 1).

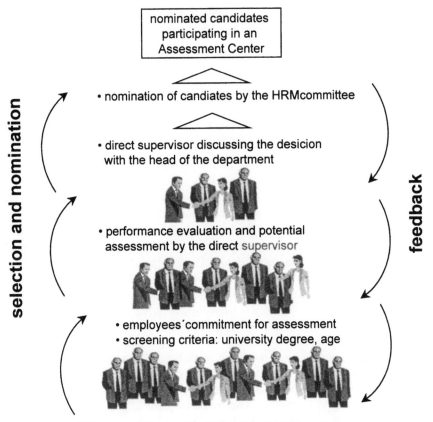

FIG. 1   The high potential selection and nomination process.

Once the nomination procedure is completed, supervisor review sessions begin. Direct supervisors give detailed feedback to all candidates about the assessments. The feedback process is guided by standardized feedback tools. These tools include a form for the preparation of the review session, guidelines for the review session itself with different feedback rules, and a commitment form documenting the results of the review session.

DIMENSIONS OF PERFORMANCE: CORE COMPETENCIES AS SELECTION CRITERIA

The company has specified company-specific core competencies that are considered to be fundamental for the highly efficient and highly competitive new generation of executives. Vision and strategic thinking, customer focus and results orientation, are some of the eight core competencies. Strategic thinking means that the employee sets a clear direction and objectives to follow. Customer focus means keeping the organization focused on understanding the needs of customers. An employee that is highly results-oriented focuses strongly on developing results for the company. The further core competencies are interpersonal skills, team development, change leadership, managing diversity, and functioning globally. The eight company-specific core competencies are used as the basic selection criteria for high potentials. It should be noted that behaviour within each core competency category can overlap into other categories.

TRAINING PROGRAMME TO IMPROVE THE ASSESSMENT PROCESS

All supervisors participate in the training programme before they take on an active role in the high potential selection procedure. The training programme clarifies the role and the tasks of the supervisors within the selection process and helps to familiarize them with the standardized assessment forms. The programme is organized by the Personnel Development and HRM Department as half-day training sessions for groups of 10 to 15 supervisors. The training deals mainly with the core competencies as they are the basis of the performance assessments. In the past the definition of the competency categories was too broad and the descriptions of the competencies were not behaviour oriented enough.

The newly developed training programme therefore provides a more detailed description and operationalization of the core competencies. Each core competency is operationalized by a number of items that describe definite behaviour patterns, e.g. the core competency "vision and strategic thinking" is operationalized by items such as "employee develops alternative solutions for problem solving", "formulates concrete future plans", "gets the priorities right ", and so on. The competency "customer focus" is described by items such as "employee identifies customer needs" and "asks regularly for feedback about customer satisfaction". The eight core competencies are operationalized by a list of 60 single items.

Part of the training programme is to familiarize the supervisors with the item list. The supervisors complete the application of the assessment categories by exemplary filling in the whole list: they are told to think of one particular employee and to judge this employee for all the performance behaviour patterns that are specified in the list. They can give ratings from "employee doesn't show that behaviour at all" to "employee shows the behaviour very often in the working situation." By working with the item list on this very specific and behaviour-oriented level, the supervisors are being sensitized to behaviour patterns shown by their employees. Their observation capabilities are improved and they get a more elaborate understanding of what is meant by the overall core competencies. A parallel can be drawn to training programmes for assessors within Assessment Centre procedures, they lead to similar results.

After training is completed the supervisors are required to give their assessments for each individual candidate according to the core competencies.

They are able to give sound assessments and can easily add examples that support the single competency-categories. Furthermore, the subtly differentiated performance profile received in the item list for each candidate helps them to give detailed feedback information to the employees within the review sessions.

EXPERIENCES WITH THE TRAINING PROGRAMME

In extended interviews after the training session, the supervisors were asked about their experiences with the training programme, and the practicability of the item list in particular. The supervisors reported that the training had sensitized them to see the selection and development of personnel as one of the supervisor's central tasks. On the whole, the item list turned out to be practicable. It took the supervisors about 20 minutes to fill in the item list for one candidate. The time needed to complete the whole assessment form for one candidate (item list plus written assessment) was about one hour, which the supervisors considered to be an appropriate amount of time.

The training ensured high transparency of the whole high potential selection process. The supervisors reported a better understanding of the core competencies after the training session. They said that they felt more competent in the whole assessment process. They had the impression that their assessments were more sound and verifiable now. The item list had helped them to observe the employees' behaviour in a well-directed and subtly differentiated manner. Additionally, the supervisors reported more sensitivity to the different behaviour facets of the employees in the everyday work process. Working with the detailed item list in the training programme had improved their general observation capability.

Furthermore, the supervisors were now able to give more detailed and structured feedback information to their employees about their performance behaviour.

In addition to these subjective ratings of the supervisors, some objective measures that prove the efficiency of the training programme are available. The HRM Department checked about 80 core competency profile forms filled in within the high potential selection process by the supervisors who had participated in the pilot training programme. There was less missing data, more detailed statements, and more elaborate examples for the candidates' behaviour in the core competency profile form after the training than in the high potential selection process the year before without the specific training programme. This indicates that the quality of the assessments has improved.

Furthermore, the number of candidates that successfully passed the assessment centre after the nomination procedure has increased. This suggests that a greater number of competent candidates have been identified in the nomination procedure.

As an overall evaluation of the training programme, it can be summarized that the observation capability of the supervisors has been improved and their assessments are nowadays sound. The experience of Opel shows that training programmes for the supervisors are worthwhile. With such training programmes the quality of the high potential selection processes can be improved and the accuracy of the assessments can be increased.

A Commentary on" Training Supervisors' Assessment Skills: A Crucial Step in High Potential Selection" by S. Remdisch and S. Dionisius

Marek Adamiec, University of Silesia, Katowice, Poland

The article came out of practical experiences, and shows the problems we meet, trying to apply more effective procedures of human resources management, in this case the assessment of high potential employees by their supervisors. The training undertaken in Adam Opel AG reminds us that the skill of evaluating and assessing people is a complicated and compound one. We must not rely on any spontaneous and "inherited" ability, but must train and develop this skill just as a skill: something learned and improving. The article shows how to do it.

In the process of training the supervisors, we meet different attitudes towards, and different possibilities of, evaluating the performance and/or the person of the employee. The aim of training should be (1) to operationalize all general, often vague concepts (dimensions, categories, etc.) used in the process and to turn them into useful, practical tools, (2) to make clear what are the most personal, subjective attitudes and views, engaged in the process of evaluation. The first task was fulfilled by the authors; in my opinion, the problem of language and understanding of concepts should be one of the most important in the training of assessment skills. The training should in a large part consist of group discussion about the meaning of terms and concepts used in the assessment. As a result, the supervisors should reach consensus: what they really do, and on what bases? This is an important social aspect of assessment procedure. I suggest the use of special case studies as a base for discussion in this part: the preparation of such "prototypical" cases would be the practical consequence of the work done.

As for the second task, an individualized approach to the trained supervisors is advised. We should implement some kind of psychological diagnosis of individual, e.g. his or her "assessment style", "cognitive style", or individual preferences in making social attributions, and then, as a result, prepare the content of the training of supervisors. We should know whom their group consist of. Are there more engineers? Economists? Managers with more humanistic background or education? This knowledge may be useful. Engineers are claimed, for example (have in mind the notion of "technical" and "humanistic" culture) to have a special type of thinking, tending to base their evaluations on measurable and strictly defined facts and principles, so perhaps they feel uneasy with the unclear and "fuzzy-set" type of matters, as is common in employee assessment (of course, not only engineers avoid making clear and sharp judgements about people—but all for the same reasons). Such individual or social biases and differences, more or less unconscious, should be revealed and discussed during training. The intended outcome of the training is to make supervisors more sensitive to the emotional and interpersonal aspects of evaluating people, and better prepared for doing it as objectively and reliably as possible. Just here I see the need for developing special psychological tool(s) for diagnosing assessors. The problem should be discussed in the context of theory of social perception and attribution and viewed as the contribution to this field.

The important issue in the article is the inevitable question: Can we prove that supervisors' training is effective? The authors applied two kinds of data for confirmation of the positive answer: first, subjective opinion of supervisors about the results of the training, and, second, checking of competency profile forms. It seems possible to use yet another measure: the opinions of employees about "feedback" given to them by their supervisors: How good (detailed, clearly formulated, useful, etc.) is it? I would name it "meta-feedback" if I weren't afraid that it's too bombastic. Nevertheless, this form of verification can be applied.

The conclusion of the article must be strongly supported: The training and developing of the assessors' skills in the field of analysing and evaluating of employees' performances is one of the fundamentals of human resources management—ensures that the real resources will be kept and developed in the organization.

A Commentary on "Training Supervisors' Assessment Skills: A Crucial Step in High Potential Selection" by S. Remdisch and S. Dionisius

Jerzy Maczynski, University of Wroclaw, Wroclaw, Poland

This paper describes the role of supervisors involved in implementing the high potential selection procedure applied at the Opel Company in Germany. The article is composed of four parts. In the first part, the authors describe different steps in the high potential selection and nomination procedures applied at Opel. We learn that the assessment procedure is done on the basis of three standardized assessment forms: "The core competencies profile form, the form for the description of accomplishment, and the final recommendation and decision form." In the second part of the paper, the authors analyse the core competencies used at Opel as the basic selection criteria for assessing high potential employees. The authors describe briefly the eight company-specific core competencies that are crucial for management effectiveness for the upcoming generation of supervisors. Among other things, the ability to function globally was identified as an important factor contributing to management effectiveness.

At this point, it would have been worthwhile for the authors to have presented more detailed evidence concerning the validity of the identified company-specific core competencies responsible for successful work performance in management positions. It would be particularly relevant in organizations faced with rapid technical change, new technologies, and which have to adapt to new challenges and requirements, given that there is increased globalization of industrial organizations, and that interdependencies have increased among nations throughout the world.

In the third section the authors discuss the content of the training programme, which is concerned with improving the assessment procedure. The authors stress, very correctly, the importance of behavioural orientation in the description and operationalization of the core competencies. The authors give some evidence to indicate how eight of the core competencies have been operationalized by the use of sixty behaviour-oriented items. Despite the fact that authors provide a detailed illustration of how the process of operationalization is implemented, the academic reader might wish to see a more sophisticated discussion of how the core competencies are measured operationally.

Finally, the authors provide evidence that, after the training session, trainees reported having come to a deeper understanding of the core competencies, and they indicated that they had acquired knowledge of, and skills for, assessing candidates for managerial positions.

The authors conclude that "with such training programmes the quality of the high potential selection processes can be improved and the accuracy of the assessments can be increased". Nevertheless, it seems that an important factor contributing to the validity of the training programme should have been more strongly supported with evidence (based on statistical analyses) that there is indeed a strong positive correlation between the outcomes of the training process and management effectiveness itself. In other words, is there any connection between training programme effects and subsequent managerial performance of those candidates identified and selected for supervisory roles? Do these candidates for managerial positions actually succeed in fulfilling the requirements of their supervisory roles after having been chosen for those positions?

Nevertheless, this article certainly provides readers with an adequate picture of the essential steps in improving the quality of the assessment procedure based on the experiences with the training programme at Opel.

EUROPEAN JOURNAL OF WORK AND ORGANIZATIONAL PSYCHOLOGY, 1998, 7 (4), 567–576

Removing Limits to Growth: Implementing Knowledge Sharing Loops between Operators and Engineers

Marinus Follon

Dow Chemical, Terneuzen, The Netherlands

The author describes the origin and the structure of the expertise of Improvement Engineers and Process Operators (Duncan, 1987). Engineers develop expertise by *deduction*: the top-down development of a production process. Operators develop expertise by *induction*: the manual intervention into a process (De Keyser, 1987). Thus the mental model of an Engineer is "abstract" and "explicit" (easy to document), while the mental model of an Operator is "concrete" and "tacit". Therefore, the author calls the expertise of Engineers *explicit knowledge* and the expertise of Operators *tacit knowledge* (Nonaka & Takeuchi, 1995). The author also describes knowledge sharing loops which capture this tacit knowledge (Operators) and incorporate it into explicit knowledge (Engineers). The process produces Knowledge Based Solutions and Most Effective Technology (MET). The deployment of MET directly generates economic profit. Knowledge Based Solutions improve the troubleshooting skills of Operators and allow Engineers to focus on the deployment of MET. This new knowledge sharing process came out of a system analysis (Senge, 1990) embedded in a bottom-up business re-engineering programme of the Styrenics Naturals Plant (SNP). Two years later, data show that this process creates value. But it is not robust. It's quickest gains are in process control and in product transitions.

ORGANISATIONAL CONTEXT

In 1995 the Dow Chemical Company started a business re-engineering pro-gramme within its Manufacturing and Engineering departments. Typically by means of a bottom-up approach Operators and/or Engineers together with a

Request for reprints should be addressed to M. Follon, Light Hydro Carbons 1, Dow Chemical, Postbus 48, 4530 AA Terneuzen, Holland; Email: mjfollon@dow.com

The author has written a first draft of this paper when he as a Process Control Engineer participated in a re-design team consisting of four Engineers (A. van de Welle, L. Govaerts, A. Pieters, M. Follon), one Operator (G. Maes) and a Facilitator (P. Martens). Without M. Clarke the ideas described in this article would never have been implemented. B. Visser, M. Clarke, and Prof. Dr. V. de Keyser (University of Liege) encouraged the author to write this article. And last but not least there is R. Vermeire. He pioneered knowledge sharing long before Nonaka and Takeuchi (1995) reinvented the concept.

skilled facilitator do an organizational redesign which contributes to the realization of a number of business stretch goals. The author reports on such a bottom-up re-engineering: the redesign of the Improvement Engineers of an SNP plant. The starting point of the design was the department's mission statement: "Engineers have to focus on the deployment of Most Effective Technology (MET)." The deployment of MET directly generates economic profit. But the reality was that Operators asked lots of troubleshooting support. Thus, the Design Team was facing a dilemma. And it didn't know how to resolve that dilemma until it made a system diagram (Senge, 1990). The system diagram revealed a new process: the knowledge sharing process between Engineers and Operators (Nonaka & Takeuchi, 1995). This process solves the previously mentioned dilemma. To explain this, three basic questions are answered in the remainder of this article:

- What type of knowledge do Engineers and Operators have to share?
- Why do Engineers and Operators have to share knowledge?
- How can Engineers and Operators share knowledge?

After this, the system diagram, and then some results and learning experiences, are discussed.

WHAT TYPE OF KNOWLEDGE DO ENGINEERS AND OPERATORS HAVE TO SHARE?

There is evidence available (Duncan, 1987; Herry 1987) that Operators and Improvement Engineers build up a different type of expertise. Engineers develop expertise by *deduction*: the top-down development of a production process. Thus, the mental model of an Engineer is relatively "abstract" and "explicit" (easy to document). Therefore the expertise of Engineers is *explicit knowledge* (Nonaka & Takeuchi, 1995). This explicit knowledge is organized into several layers of abstraction. When an Engineer explains the "why?" of design decision to Operators, he flexibly swaps between those layers of abstraction. Abstraction layers to be shared are (Wirstad, 1988):

Functional Meaning (the highest level of abstraction). A production process is seen as part of an environment from which it receives some inputs and in which it injects some outputs. Relevant knowledge structures relate to the interrelations between production trains and between plans.

Functional Structure. A production process is seen as a network between process variables. Knowledge structures relevant for sharing with Operators are:

- knowledge of mass and energy balances
- knowledge of process functions of unit operations, the "should-be" operating conditions and "the why?" of those operating conditions
- knowledge of high level control strategy
- knowledge of the chemical properties of products.

Physical Function. A production process is seen as a network between physical units (major equipment, pumps, valves, etc.). Knowledge structures relevant for sharing with Operators are:

- knowledge of MET (most effective technology)
- knowledge of MLTCO (minimum long-term costs of ownership)
- knowledge of controller modes (the "why" of the controller modes).

An Operator develops his or her expertise by *induction*: the manual intervention into the process. It is his or her own action feedback (e.g. was the previous intervention successful or not) which shapes diagnostic skills and the model of the process. Thus, the mental model of an Operator is relatively "concrete" and "tacit". That is why this expertise is *tacit knowledge*. This dependency on action feedback also shows the irony with the automation of (petro)chemical plants: The designer who tries to eliminate the operator still leaves the operator to do the tasks the designer does not know how to eliminate cost effectively. As a consequence the operator is left with an arbitrary collection of tasks, and little help is given to develop the skills to handle those tasks (Bainbridge, 1987). Tacit knowledge of Operators relevant to be shared with Engineers is (De Keyser, 1987; Wirstad, 1988):

- knowledge of actual operating conditions
- knowledge of physical plant lay-out, e.g. location of major equipment, pumps and control valves
- knowledge of components, e.g. function, construction, capacity, limitations, inputs, and outputs of major equipment/pumps/valves
- knowledge of localizing and identifying disturbances and knowledge on how causes of malfunction propagate through a plant. This is called *diagnostic knowledge*: the knowledge to derive from a pattern of symptoms one or more causes. In dynamic systems, diagnostic problems can be very complex. Those complexities can be caused by the separation in time of symptom and cause ("referred symptoms"). As an example, in a complex reactor distillation configuration reactor heat is transferred to a distillation tower; the reactor develops a fault; the first symptoms might not first appear in the reactor instrumentation, but in the boil-up of the distillation column.

- knowledge of measures at disturbances. An operator can only effectively intervene when he or she: (1) knows both the procedure to be executed and "the why?" of this procedure; (2) has a good understanding of timing aspects and has *integrated* them into his or her action repertoire:
  - trajectory over time of interacting process units
  - what is the speed with which a certain type variation entails an accident or stoppage (this is not a matter of clock time but of action time)
  - notion of duration of operations
  - chronology of actions
  - intervention time, e.g. How much time do I need for this action; e.g. How long does it take before this action has effect on a particular process variable?

  and (3) can operate in feed-forward mode. This means that he or she can anticipate physical phenomena.

WHY DO ENGINEERS AND OPERATORS HAVE TO SHARE KNOWLEDGE?

Engineers and Operators have to share knowledge because the process produces Most Effective Technology (MET) and Knowledge Based Solutions.

MET. This is distinguished from Best Available Technology (BAT). It focuses on economic value, standardization and has incorporated the expertise of Process Operators. The deployment of MET directly generates economic profit. As an example, a control template for a major unit operation (a distillation tower, a furnace, etc.), will only be most effective if it has incorporated the temporal reasoning of the Operators. When Engineers automate start-up procedures, they tend to focus on causal time and clock time. Causal time relates to process states which must be successively realized to make the unit operation fully operational. Clock time relates to the measuring of time (the time between the boil-up of a distillation tower and its flooding). Engineers deduce this causal time and clock time from abstract process models. Very often those start-up procedures are cumbersome for Operators: they ignore the expertise of Operators which integrates causal time and clock time with logical time. Logical time refers to the consistent, logical action repertoire of Operators to handle expected and unexpected events (equipment break down, instrumentation failure, recovering human error, etc.). De Keyser (1995) describes how the expertise of Operators integrates several temporal reference systems.

Knowledge Based Solutions. These don't require much capital. They improve the troubleshooting skills of Operators and allow Engineers to focus on the deployment of MET. Performance Indicators are examples of Knowledge Based Solutions. They show Operators in a glance the status of a production process and help them to become more proactive in their control of the process (Goodstein, 1981). A Performance Indicator is depicted as a circle whose colour is determined by high level process calculations (mass and energy balances). It is also a navigation marker: If the Operator clicks on it, a process flowsheet is launched showing the cause of the distorted mass and energy balance (if there is a distortion). Engineers can not develop those Performance Indicators alone: they just don't have the right expertise to know to which flowsheet you have to navigate to solve the problem. Operators do have this expertise, but they can not calculate mass and energy balances. It is the author's own experience that Operators tend to develop too many Performance Indicators and flowsheets. This creates a maintenance problem and a standardization problem. That is why Operators and Engineers have to share knowledge.

Knowledge Sharing.   By knowledge sharing Operators and Engineers also learn a great deal from each other. Engineers become aware of their lack of knowledge of the actual operating conditions of the plant. They start to realize the difficulties Operators have to face when they have to monitor or diagnose the trajectory over time of interacting process units. Operators learn a great deal about the correct behaviour of the process, the process functions of the unit operations, their control intent, and high level control strategy (De Keyser, 1987).

HOW DO ENGINEERS AND OPERATORS SHARE KNOWLEDGE?

Figure 1 depicts the process of knowledge sharing as a control (feedback) loop.

SYSTEM DIAGRAM

When we restrict the system diagram (Senge, 1990) to manufacturing, it consists of three loops.

The Dominant Loop—between the Engineers and the Technology Implementation Process.   Because this loop makes money, all limiting factors for growth should be removed. Two factors make this loop work as a snowball (in successive iterations it swallows more and more resources):

• The Technology Implementation Process is very structured. It is based on a strict step diagram and results in projects with clearly defined economic profits, deadlines, and results measurements. The compensation of the Improvement Engineers depends for a large part on the success of their projects. All this injects a lot of energy in this loop.

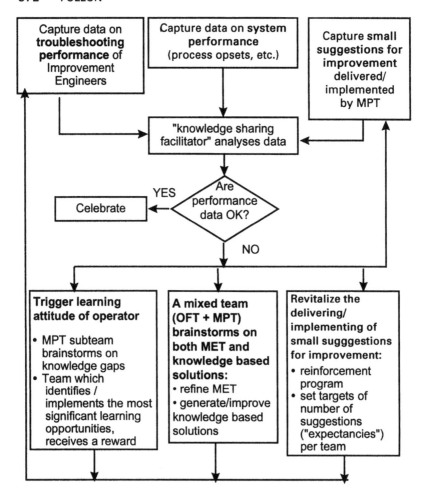

FIG. 1.   Knowledge sharing depicted as a control loop.

• The Technology Implementation Process prioritizes on the basis of the economic profit of single unit suggestions. As such it reinforces a culture which celebrates the delivering of a "big bang" technology plan, and which discourages the delivering of a great number of smaller suggestions for improvement (so called "trivial" suggestions for improvement). The economic profit of a "trivial" suggestion is not significant, though the cumulative benefit of an avalanche of small suggestions could be huge (Nonaka & Takeuchi, 1995).

Because in this system this loop works as a snowball it can easily kill the two other loops.

The second loop is the knowledge sharing loop—between Engineers and the Manage Production Process (Operators).   To make this loop stronger we make somebody responsible: the Knowledge Sharing Facilitation Role.

The third loop—between Engineers and the Manage&Transfer Technology Process. The Improvement Engineers receive MET/Knowledge Based Solutions from their business and send back suggestions for improvement. If this feedback loop is killed, the expertise of Operators will never be distributed across the globe. To make this loop stronger Engineers should know:

- the MET/Knowledge Based Solutions the globe is interested in
- the owners of MET/Knowledge Based Solutions to whom they can send their improvements
- the "expectancies" of the globe: targets of numbers of MET/Knowledge Based Solutions
- the "go/no go" decision of their suggestions for improvement (quick feedback is important)
- a reinforcement plan boosting the motivation to disseminate MET/Knowledge Based Solutions.

As a conclusion we state that Engineers will only realize strong value creation if they succeed in keeping all the three loops running. The big challenge is to combine a rapid implementation of MET with a number of small steps: gradually reducing troubleshooting support (Knowledge Based Solutions), improving MET, and disseminating MET/Knowledge Based Solutions across the globe. The three loops are illustrated in Fig. 2.

RESULTS AND LEARNING EXPERIENCES
TWO YEARS AFTER THE INITIAL DESIGN

Figure 3 shows that the system diagram produced "double loop learning" (Argyris, 1977).

Data show that those new knowledge sharing loops create value for the Terneuzen SNP: Recently a Design Team of Operators developed a new staffing concept for the production process. Contributing to their proposal to reduce shift size was the fact that the Knowledge Based Solutions have significantly improved the troubleshooting skills of the Operators.

The visible support of Plant Leadership is a key enabler to make a bottom-up approach a success (Frohman, 1992). The pilot in the SNP recognized and realized this requirement. During the design and the implementation the Plant Production Leader frequently expressed his recognition for the work the design team did. He was always available to help to remove barriers.

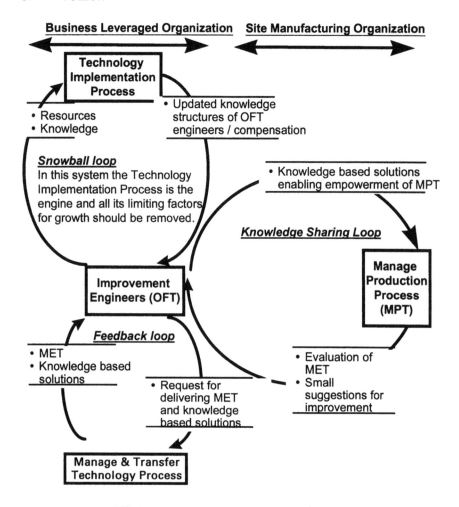

FIG. 2.   System diagram of improvement engineers.

A system analysis needs to be more than a intellectual analysis of an inter-ventionist. It has to trigger relational and learning processes (Checkland, 1981). By embedding a system analysis into a bottom-up approach the pilot realized this second requirement. The system analysis cost a lot of discussion and emotional energy. This investment paid for itself because it facilitated the development of a shared vision (the Design Team members sounded all design decisions with their own group) and the commitment of Engineers, Operators, and Leaders to implement those concepts.

The quickest gains of knowledge sharing are in process control and in product transitions. Nevertheless it was not the design intent to restrict knowledge

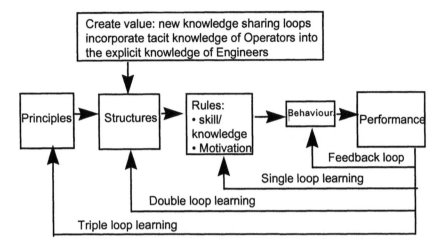

FIG. 3.   Three levels of learning (Argyris 1977) applied in design SNP.

sharing to one particular discipline: for example process engineering also needs the expertise of Operators. Recently a top consultant in process engineering has remarked that those new knowledge sharing concepts have touched the right chord. He admitted that, throughout his career, process control engineers have have been closer to the plant than process engineers. Process engineers alone can not cope anymore with the galloping technologies. The role calls for a positive and fundamental reappraisal (see also Duncan, 1987).

The Knowledge Sharing Facilitation Role is not a robust role. It's requirements are very demanding: plant process knowledge, facilitation skills, understanding the expertise of Operators, and last but not least being accepted both by Operators and Engineers. There aren't many Engineers who possess all those skills. That is why the knowledge sharing process implodes if that particular Engineer is ill or is not available for a while due to high workload. The solution is to consider it not as a permanent role but to plan it for a few days each month.

REFERENCES

Argyris, C. (1977). Double loop learning in organizations. *Harvard Business Review*, 115–124.

Bainbridge, L. (1987). Ironies of automation. In J. Rasmussen, K. Duncan, & J. Leplat (Eds), *New technology and human error*. Chichester: John Wiley & Sons.

Checkland, P. (1981). *Systems thinking, systems practice*. Chichester: John Wiley & Sons.

De Keyser, V. (1987). Structuring of knowledge of operators in continuous processes. In J. Rasmussen, K. Duncan, & J. Leplat (Eds), *New technology and human error*. Chichester: John Wiley & Sons.

De Keyser, V. (1995). Time in ergonomics research. *Ergonomics*, *38*(8), 1639–1660.

Duncan, K. (1987). Reflections on fault diagnostic expertise. In J. Rasmussen, K. Duncan, & J. Leplat (Eds), *New technology and human error*. Chichester: John Wiley & Sons.

Frohman, A. (1992). *Middle management challenge: Moving from crisis to empowerment*. New York: McGraw-Hill.

Goodstein, L. (1981). Discrimative display support for process operators. In J. Rasmussen & W. Rouse (Eds), *Human detection and diagnosis of system failures*. New York: Plenum Press.

Herry, N. (1987). Errors in the execution of prescribed instructions. In J. Rasmussen, K. Duncan, & J. Leplat (Eds), *New technology and human error*. Chichester: John Wiley & Sons.

Nonaka, I., & Takeuchi, H. (1995). *The knowledge creating company*. New York: Oxford University Press.

Senge, P. (1990). *The fifth discipline*. New York: Doubleday.

Wirstad, J. (1988). On knowledge structures for process operators. In L. Goodstein, H. Andersen, & S. Olsen (Eds), *Tasks, errors and mental models*. New York: Taylor & Francis.

A Commentary on "Removing Limits to Growth: Implementing Knowledge Sharing Loops between Operators and Engineers" by M. Follon

Virginijus Lepeska, Vilnius University, Vilnius, Lithuania

In his article, Marinus Follon describes team learning experience at the Terneuzen Styrenics Naturals plant using knowledge sharing between two different professional groups of the employees. The programme has been started with a very practical purpose—to improve decision-making quality and develop technologies. The project was developed and implemented by practitioners—members of the organization. At the same time, scientific basis of the programme is evident. For example, the knowledge sharing process is described by using concepts of Argyris and Senge's theoretical models.

The practice described specifies the understanding of team learning process in organizations. The case proves the impact of knowledge sharing to improvement of competitiveness of the organization and problem-solving skills of the employees. It appeared that the knowledge sharing process provided enrichment of the mental models of both engineers and operators: Engineers gained awareness of 'down to earth' aspect of the operating conditions of the plant and operators gained broader perspective of the operational processes. Limiting factors affecting knowledge sharing process and its results were defined.

A few aspects of knowledge sharing process have been mentioned which might be interesting topics for further research in the area. Broader aspects of the effects of knowledge sharing process might be investigated in greater depth. The conditions of successful implementation of the process (such as ways of managing the motivation of employees to participate in the knowledge sharing process and the most effective procedures of the process) might be elaborated on and described in more detail.

Marinus Follon's article is an encouraging example of describing the rich experience of how team learning affects the organization. Data from the field are needed that provide the possibility to test and enrich theoretical models and concepts.

EUROPEAN JOURNAL OF WORK AND ORGANIZATIONAL PSYCHOLOGY, 1998, 7 (4), 579–581

Book Review

Spencer, L.M., & Spencer, S.M. (1993). *Competence* at *work: Models for superior performance.* New York: Wiley. Pp. 384. ISBN 0-471-54809-X. £70.00.

The identification of factors explaining superior performance at work has been acknowledged as a topic of great importance by the majority of enterprises, thus partly contributing to the fact that this domain became a focus of psychological research. Spencer and Spencer's competency approach takes the discussion of outstanding performance from a behavioural point of view; starting with the assessment of successful work outcomes, competencies that are involved in them are examined.

The book presents a sound overall view of 20 years of research using the McClelland/McBer job competence assessment (JCA) instruments. The authors' aims are: (1) to summarize the studies and the competencies found to contribute to superior performance, (2) to give a guide as to how to carry out JCA studies, (3) to describe the implications of the results for human resource management applications, and (4) to suggest future applications for competency research. The target groups are human resource professionals and managers who could help individuals and organizations to improve their level of performance, by assessing and training individual competencies and their fit to job requirements. Composed of five main parts, the book gives a comprehensive overview of the con-ceptualization process inherent to the study and implementation of the competency approach.

Starting with an introduction by David McClelland, whose publication "Testing for competence rather than intelligence" (1973) may be seen as the initiation of competency research, Part 1 defines competency as "an *underlying characteristic* of an individual that is *causally related to criterion-referenced effective and/or superior performance* in a job or a situation" (p. 9, original emphasis). Underlying characteristics of personality predicting behaviour in a variety of situations split up into five different types: the "central" competencies of motives, traits, and self-concept on the one hand, and the "surface" com-petencies of knowledge and skills on the other. The causal relationship of competencies implies that they predict skilled behaviour, which in turn predicts job performance outcomes. The criterion reference assures that competencies correspond to real job standards. The main aspects of competency research are: (1) the analysis of successful work outcomes, (2) criterion sampling (assessment of correlates of effective performance by comparing people having success in their job with other people who do not), and (3) assessment of skills causally related to successful outcomes.

A competency dictionary is developed in Part 2 which also suggests criteria for the competencies that predict outstanding performance. Competency clusters drawn from empirical observations are defined on the basis of underlying motives. Part 3 gives instructions for designing competency studies by presenting three alternative methods: A design using criterion samples, a design using expert panels, and a design for studies of single jobs which do not have enough jobholders to offer criterion samples. Part 4 summarizes the findings in the form of generic competency models, which provide a general framework for the study of outstanding performance in a variety of occupational settings: Technical professionals, salespeople, helping and human service workers, and managers. Finally, specific entrepreneur assessment methods are developed on the basis of the data issued of cross-cultural studies.

The fifth and most important part illustrates the use of competency data in human resource management applications such as selection, performance management, career and succession planning, development, and compensation systems. A solid overview presents conditions and methods for competency assessment and the implementation of a competency-based system in human resource management. Concrete examples illustrate the proceedings together with possible results. Future directions for competency research are developed. A very good point made by the authors is to highlight the importance of person–job fits as a necessary goal of the implementation of competency-based systems. Conclusively, one could say that a relatively small number of competencies are required and should be developed in educational as well as professional settings: achievement orientation, initiative, information seeking, conceptual thinking, interpersonal understanding, self-confidence, impact and influence, and collaborativeness.

As a general evaluation, one could say that the authors offer an excellent overview of the competency approach as a field of organizational practice as well as a domain of research. The book provides sound arguments to support the inclusion of the competency approach in organizational development. The main contribution consists in the precise methodological information which is given about competency assessment instruments and training methods. Of special interest is the detailed description of developing a competency dictionary on the basis of empirical observations, which may be highly useful for organizational practices as well as research projects. This dictionary presents competencies in generic form, in scales designed to cover behaviour in a wide range of jobs, and to be adapted for many applications; this of course makes the instrument unspecific at the same time. The lack of references for the investigation methods represents one negative point. For carrying out studies in the domain of outstanding performance, the reader might miss the theoretical framework and the empirical confirmation of some methods.

Which results can be achieved by relating the competency approach to expertise studies? It appears essential that research in the domains of competency and of expertise benefit from each other in order to create a comprehensive theoretical framework of outstanding performance. The book contributes to this framework to the extent that the conceptualization and methodology of the competency approach may provide useful hints for the operationalization of expertise within professional settings (e.g. for peer nomination methods or superiors' ratings of the degree of expertise). As a matter of fact, the steps proposed within the classic competency study design are very similar in studies of professional expertise: definition of performance effectiveness criteria, identification of superior and average performers, collection of data, and identification of correlates of outstanding in comparison to average performance. However, only few of the actual publications in the domain of expertise are quoted in spite of the fact that expertise research could provide fruitful theoretical foundations to the competency approach and its practical implications. Expertise studies may complete the competency approach in the sense that they do not only investigate cognitive and motivational predictors in a distinctive way, but also the underlying processes of outstanding performance.

McClelland, D.C. (1973). Testing for competence rather than intelligence. *American Psychologist, 46*(10), 1–14.

JEANETTE HRON
Institut für Psychologie, Organisations- und Wirtschaftspsychologie,
München, Germany.

THE EUROPEAN JOURNAL OF WORK AND ORGANIZATIONAL PSYCHOLOGY, 1998, *7*(4) 582–589

PROFESSIONAL NEWS SECTION
John Toplis, Editor

CONTENTS

Copy and information for the Professional News Section should be sent to: John Toplis, Employee Development Manager, Royal Mail Anglia, The Vineyards, Great Baddow, Chelmsford, Essex CM99 1AA. Telephone 01245 243189; Fax 01245 243062; Email: John.Toplis@btinternet.com The Section Editor's views are not necessarily those of the British Post Office or of Royal Mail.

INTRODUCTION TO THE PROFESSIONAL NEWS SECTION
John Toplis

Welcome to the first Professional News Section of 1999.

It would be good if 1999 were to be a year of world-wide peace and prosperity, setting the scene for a good start to the millennium. But as I write this at the beginning of November 1998, neither peace nor prosperity are assured. So far as peace is concerned, there remain a large number of trouble spots around the world, ranging from Afghanistan and East Timor; closer to home, the peace processes in both the Middle East and Northern Ireland have yet to be resolved.

So far as prosperity is concerned, the G7 leaders have now agreed an action plan for saving the planet—including the establishment of a £90

---

billion credit line to help troubled nations. The British newspaper, *The Sunday Business*, comments: "exactly how close the world economies came to the brink we may never know."

During the time I was involved with the Business Education Programme within the British Post Office, guest speakers talked in terms of global businesses and alliances. Participants became aware of the potential impact of competitors from overseas, not just in overseas markets, but in the UK as well. This thinking seems somewhat at odds with the views of some that it may be possible to isolate the economies of America and Europe from the depression now being experienced by much of the rest of the world.

Some commentators believe that overcapacity is the fundamental cause of the current economic difficulties, and it will be interesting to see whether psychologists can help companies to retain or even build market share in the face of ever-increasing competition. So far as consumer products are concerned, there are renewed signs that aesthetics can be a factor in consumer choice—motoring journalists will comment about the feeling of quality given by the sound of a car door closing, while the appearances of the latest Apple computers and of the new Nokia phones are further examples. Nokia are now the world-wide market leaders in mobile phones, a remarkable achievement for a company based in rural Finland.

The European Journal of Work and Organizational Psychology devoted a special issue to Innovation in Organizations (Volume 5, Number 1) and the work if psychologists in running focus groups to help evaluate products is relatively well known. But it would be interesting to receive articles about other ways in which psychologists are involved in consumer product design.

This edition has one article on the SHL / UMIST Research Centre, written by Ivan Robertson and Militza Callinan. I have more than a passing interest in this article, as I am a member of the advisory committee for the new Centre.

I hope that you find the article interesting. However, if you feel (as I do) that this Professional News Section needs to have more articles from the rest of Europe, please do send me your contributions.

SHL/ UMIST RESEARCH CENTRE IN WORK AND ORGANIZATIONAL PSYCHOLOGY
Ivan Robertson and Militza Callinan

A new research centre in work and organizational psychology was established on October 1st 1997 at Manchester School of Management, UMIST, in the UK. The creation of the Centre was initiated by the Director, Ivan Robertson, who is Professor of Occupational Psychology at Manchester School of Management and Pro-Vice Chancellor at UMIST. So far, considerable success has been achieved. Substantial financial support has been attracted from sources such as the European Regional Development Fund, academic, and commercial sponsors. The Centre now has six members of staff, in addition to the Director, working on 4 major projects, with further work currently being developed. Brief details of the main projects are outlined below.

The aim of the Centre is to provide a focal point for international research, expertise and opinion on the psychological factors that influence people's effectiveness and well-being at work. Some basic criteria are applied to work at the Centre. Most importantly, the research must be progressive: It must promise the creation of new understanding by asking novel and challenging questions. The Centre aims to be progressive not only in the content of the work but also in the form of the projects. Novel or uncommon forms of partnership will be positively sought where they have the potential to create more innovative solutions or enhanced understanding. Possible partners will be both research and commercial psychologists, but also researchers from other disciplines and those inside organizations. The intended result is high quality research that is both scientifically interesting and has a significant impact for organizations.

The collaboration behind the establishment of the Centre is itself a little unprecedented. It was established with core sponsorship from SHL Group plc. Most commercial sponsorship in the field is for work confined to addressing specific, well-defined and demonstrably market-focused questions. In this case, the funds support the central running costs of the Centre rather than specific research activity. The research itself is not constrained in any way by the need to demonstrate direct benefits in relation to the core sponsor's commercial objectives. In fact, it is likely that most of the research will not have direct or immediate commercial relevance. Each piece of research is

Requests for reprints should be addressed to Militza Callinan, SHL/UMIST Research Centre in Work and Organisational Psychology, Manchester School of Management, UMIST, PO Box 88, Manchester M60 1QD.

autonomous and self-funding, which allows each project to be developed and evaluated in relation to the scientific and practical objectives of the particular partners involved.

By contributing to the necessary resources that allow the Centre to develop innovative working partnerships and leading-edge research, SHL will benefit in a more expansive, and ultimately, a more profitable way. The benefit is that the Centre will contribute to the development of the field of work and organizational psychology into one that can and does demonstrate that it is a relevant and fundamental component in the basic design and management of work and organizations. All of us, whatever our particular focus, will benefit from the value of our discipline becoming more widely recognized and employed.

Economics and marketing, for example, are seen as essential knowledge areas and key considerations in the forming of an organization's strategy and operations. By contrast, psychological issues are rarely viewed as crucial to bottom-line success or failure. There may be difficulties in linking some aspects of psychologists' work with overall company performance, as John Toplis notes in the last Professional News Section (September, 1998) with regards to training evaluation. In other areas though, psychological knowledge can be clearly linked with effectiveness. For example, of the high proportion of mergers and acquisitions that fail, costing millions of pounds and many jobs, evidence suggests that a third to a half can be attributed to 'employee problems' (Cartwright & Cooper, 1993).

Call centres are a further topical instance where psychological practices could be demonstrably related to a company's bottom-line. The attention of call-centre operators has been largely focused on utilizing sophisticated and expensive technologies and establishing the key factors relevant to the choice of location. Having made massive investments, call-centre managers are being faced with 'old' problems in showing a return from their 'new' environments—high staff turnover, low employee motivation, and the difficulty of measuring the quality, as well as the quantity of work performance (e.g. Welch, 1997).

Just these two examples demonstrate the interactive nature of organizations' decisions about strategy, finance, technology, and people, and so provide the justification for a holistic approach. As psychologists, we understand this without frequent reminders. It is not always the case, however, that we practice holistic approaches to organizational problems any more than the accountants that plan takeovers without considering the crucial influence that the company's employees might have on the outcome. The fact that business people do not automatically see how psychology can help them meet their objectives means that the burden of explanation and persuasion may be greater for our profession than for others. Psychologists must explain and persuade, however, if the field is to gain more opportunities to demonstrate the impact it can have in areas traditionally inhabited by other professions. Even in familiar areas such as selection and assessment, understandable and persuasive communication would not be wasted. Conversely, we must also be prepared to recognize the relevance and importance of knowledge other than our own.

Of course, there are always cynics. Cynicism, however, is not always productive and is often restrictive. Working successfully across boundaries, whether they are between researchers and practitioners, across disciplines or across nations, requires open-mindedness. Differences in the nature or emphasis of interests for each party will demand flexibility in the criteria and objectives that are chosen in joint projects, as well as the determination to debate and resolve conflicts. Most of all, though, it requires active attempts to engage in projects that provide potential opportunities for successful collaboration. The Centre is committed to creating and engaging in such opportunities to increase the recognition, and expand the domain of psychologists in the workplace.

Meeting these aims of progressiveness and collaboration will depend, by definition, on the involvement and contribution of our colleagues across Europe and beyond. The Centre actively seeks participation, from the exchange of ideas and understanding, through to full-blown collaborative research projects. Opportunity has led to a UK bias in our current work. For this reason, international input would be particularly welcome.

If you would like to speak to us at the Centre about our current research or future plans please contact:

Director: Professor Ivan Robertson
Tel: +44 (0) 161 200 3443
Fax: +44 (0) 161 200 3518
Email: Ivan.Robertson@umist.ac.uk

Assistant Director: Militza Callinan
Tel: +44 (0) 161 200 8986
Fax: +44 (0) 161 200 8985
Email: Militza.Callinan@umist.ac.uk

Visit our web site at: http://www.umist.ac.uk/~webshl/

REFERENCES

Cartwright, S., & Cooper, C.L. (1993). The psychological impact of merger and acquisition on the individual: A study of building society managers. *Human Relations, 46,* 327–347.

Toplis, J. (1998). More about training evaluation. *European Journal of Work and Organizational Psychology, 7,* 440–441.

Welch, J. (1997). Call centres in crisis over staff shortages. *People Management, 3,* 9.

CURRENT PROJECTS

Audit and validation of the selection practices of small- and medium-sized companies

Project Directors: Professor Ivan Robertson and Dr Mike Smith (Senior Lecturer in Occupational Psychology, Manchester School of Management)

The recruitment practices of smaller firms have not so far received much attention from work psychologists. These companies may recruit few people infrequently, but the impact on the business of getting the right staff is likely to be great. The two Project Officers are working with company owners and managers to highlight areas of staff recruitment that could be improved. Importantly, they also offer practical suggestions and advice about how those improvements can be achieved. This is one of a number of projects at Manchester School of Management funded by the European Regional Development Fund to help businesses in North West England.

Project Officers: Liz Walley and Adrian Nelson. Tel: +44 (0)161 200 8984.

The influence of personality factors on customers' perceptions of service quality

Project Directors: Professor Ivan Robertson and Dr Barbara Lewis (Senior Lecturer in Marketing, Manchester School of Management)

Many organizations invest heavily in the measurement of customer satisfaction with the service provided. The resulting information is often highly influential in the development of customer care and retention strategies and operations. Research in occupational psychology has shown that certain affective reactions, (e.g. job satisfaction), are predictable, in part, from the personality characteristics of the person.

This project focuses on the hypothesis that people's reactions to services, like people's reactions to jobs, are influenced by their psychological characteristics. The potential implications, should personality factors predict quality perceptions, are important. Information about customers' views gained from instruments such as the widely used measure of service quality, SERVQUAL, may be incomplete and insufficient as a basis for guiding organizational activity. Attention will need to be given to refining these measures to exclude the influence of personality and encompass only aspects of the service provided.

Research Assistants: Philip Bardzil and Ioannis Nikolaou. Tel: +44 (0)161 200 8786.

Personality traits and situations as predictors of work behaviour
Project Director: Professor Ivan Robertson

The role of personality in describing, explaining and predicting behaviour has regained prominence in recent years. Within work and organizational psychology, the validity of personality measures for predicting significant variance in job performance has been demonstrated in a large number of studies across a wide range of people and jobs. Important advances in trait psychology have led to the emergence of five key traits, the big five, as the universal structure of human personality. Now, however, research in the field has hit a ceiling both theoretically and practically. Without incorporating features of the situation—another important influence on behaviour—the predictive validity of personality will always be constrained. New work in social psychology has also drawn attention to the possible processes by which traits are expressed as particular reactions by people in response to their environments.

This research aims to develop and test specific hypotheses of relationships between personality traits and behaviour within the framework of a theoretical model. The model will incorporate and specify the relations between: (a) the five factor model of personality trait structure; (b) the within-person organization of personality-related cognitions and affects; and (c) the salient situational features related to behavioural choice. Increased validity of prediction using personality measures has significant implications both for scientific progress and for the accuracy of practical applications, such as personnel selection and assessment instruments.
Researcher: Militza Callinan. Tel: +44 (0)161 200 8986

An investigation of the individual factors related to continued involvement in employment of people up to and beyond retirement age and its effect on psychological well-being
Project Director: Professor Ivan Robertson. Project Advisor: Professor Peter Warr (Institute of Work Psychology, Sheffield)

An ageing population means a future shortage of younger employees and an increase in the number and proportion of older workers in many developed countries. Consequently, issues relating to older people's participation in the workforce are currently receiving much attention from those concerned with social and economic policies, as well as human resource professionals.

The research being developed will explore potential differences in the personality and characteristics of older people who want to maintain some involvement in paid employment and those who do not. In particular, the interaction between people's circumstances and characteristics will be explored. Additionally, the relationship between working beyond retirement age and psychological well-being will be investigated.

This knowledge is needed to inform the development of soundly based human resource policies and practices that both include and effectively utilize the skills and experience of the growing number of older workers. The findings also have the potential to contribute to efforts at understanding the key elements of quality of life at older ages. *Contact: Militza Callinan. Tel: +44 (0)161 200 8986*

The extent and effect of inaccuracy in applicants' self-reports in employee selection
Project Director: Professor Ivan Robertson

Mistakes in the selection and recruitment of employees can have devastating consequences. Punishing costs related to poor performance, turnover and re-recruitment may be the result for the organization. Selection errors can also result in vulnerable people being subjected to physical or mental distress when inappropriate people are allowed into positions of trust. Dissimulation, or 'faking' by job applicants, intended to impress or to deliberately mislead prospective employers, is one factor that may lead to such errors.

Most research to date has focused on one type of inaccuracy and one selection method. That is, socially desirable responding and personality assessment. Research is being developed that aims to investigate the extent and effect of inaccurate applicant information across the most commonly used selection methods—CVs, application forms, and interviews—as well as personality assessment. The project will also attempt to develop more sophisticated conceptualization and measurement of dissimulation than has been used previously. Empirical data and increased understanding on this subject will be extremely valuable to recruiters in helping them decide between people by informing more effective and justifiable selection practices that take account of dissimulation on the basis of real evidence. *Contact: Militza Callinan. Tel: +44 (0)161 200 8986*

European Journal of Work and Organizational Psychology
Volume 7, 1998, Contents

Issue 3: The Individual and the Organization

Guest Editors: Gert Graversen and Jan A. Johansson

Issue 4: Expertise at Work

Guest Editors: Sabine Sonnentag and Ute Schmidt-Braße

EUROPEAN JOURNAL OF WORK AND ORGANIZATIONAL PSYCHOLOGY, VOLUME 7, 1998 AUTHOR INDEX